Reflect on the Qur'an

Mirza Yawar Baig

ISBN: 1494280361

ISBN-13: 978-1494280369

Table of Contents

Preface

Many a time some young person comes to me saying, 'Please make dua for me. I want to memorize the Qur'an.' Many a time have I had some young parent come to me asking, 'Please make dua for my child. I want him/her to become a Haafidh.' But in all these years I have yet to hear someone say, 'Please make dua for me. I want to understand the Qur'an. I want to live by the Qur'an.' Which leads me to question our understanding of even the word Haafidh (protector). True it is that the one who memorizes the Qur'an is a Haafidh. But what if all that he is really the Haafidh of, is the sound of the Ayaat – not their meaning or implementation? What therefore must we call such a person, who has memorized the sound but has no clue what it means? To make a long story short, this is the state of the majority of people who memorize the Qur'an today, especially in countries of the Indian subcontinent.

So why was the Qur'an revealed? Was it revealed so that we could memorize its sound and then live our lives any way we like? Or did it come so that we understand it, reflect on it and live our lives according to it? Let us see what the author of the Qur'an said about this. Allahﷻ said:

أَفَلَا يَتَدَبَّرُونَ الْقُرْآنَ أَمْ عَلَى قُلُوبٍ أَقْفَالُهَا

***Muhammad* 47: 24.** *Do they not* then *think deeply in the Qur'an, or are their hearts locked up (from understanding it)?*

Allahﷻ mentioned reflecting on the Qur'an and called those who don't do that, people whose hearts are locked up. I know that this Ayah came for the disbelievers but I wonder what we will say if Allahﷻ asks us this same question.

There are 228 ayaat in which Allahﷻ mentioned His Book but not in a single one of them did He say that it is sufficient to memorize its sound without understanding it and living by it. So how do we justify not only doing this but insisting that it is not necessary for a Haafidh to learn the meaning of what he is reciting and even worse, our claim that if he learns the meaning, he will not be able to memorize. How then did the Sahaba memorize? Do we ask ourselves this?

The Sahaba of Rasoolullahﷺ, the generation that Allahﷻ created to be role models for the rest of mankind until the last day, exemplified the ideal approach to the Qur'an. As we are aware, Abdullah ibn Omar ibn Al Khattabرضي الله عنه said about his (and his companions') way of learning the Qur'an, 'We used to take ten Ayaat from Rasoolullahﷺ. Then we would memorize them, understand them from him, reflect on them, act upon them and only when we were satisfied would we go to him for the next ten.' This shows where the focus was, on application and implementation in life – not merely on reading and memorizing. That is why he took twelve years to memorize Sura Al- Baqara whereas it is normal in our Hifdh Madaaris for an average student to memorize the whole Qur'an in two years.

It is with the intention of drawing attention to this great disservice to the Qur'an and harm that we do to ourselves that I decided to do this series of Juma lectures, which have been compiled into this small book. Using Sura Al-Fatiha I have tried to touch upon the wealth of knowledge and benefit that is offered to us, which for the most part, thanks to our wrong approach we lose out.

It is my hope that this will enable us to wake up and value the Qur'an as the living Word of a Living God – Allah ﷻ - besides whom there are no gods and nobody worthy of worship. What a tragedy that He sent His message but we can't take the trouble to try to understand it, even though we pay lip service to it and honor it in speech.

Let us fear the day about which Allah ﷻ warned us when none other than Rasoolullah ﷺ himself will complain about us to Allah ﷻ and say:

وَقَالَ الرَّسُولُ يَا رَبِّ إِنَّ قَوْمِي اتَّخَذُوا هَذَا الْقُرْآنَ مَهْجُورًا

Furqan 25: 30. *And the Messenger (Muhammad ﷺ) will say: "O my Rabb! Verily, my people deserted this Qur'an*

It is my hope that with the right approach instead of us memorizing the sound and calling ourselves Haafidh, if we approach the Qur'an correctly and memorize it, understand it and live by it such that the Qur'an will become our Haafidh. That in the end is the most valuable of all things.

Yawar Baig

Reflect on the Qur'an

My dear Brothers and Sisters, Ramadan is the month of the Qur'an. Allahﷻ said:

شَهْرُ رَمَضَانَ الَّذِيَ أُنزِلَ فِيهِ الْقُرْآنُ هُدًى لِّلنَّاسِ وَبَيِّنَاتٍ مِّنَ الْهُدَى وَالْفُرْقَانِ

***Baqara* 2:185.** *The month of Ramadan in which was revealed the Qur'an, a guidance for mankind and clear proofs for the guidance and the criterion (between right and wrong).*

Since it is the month of the Qur'an we listen to the Kalaam of Allahﷻ in Taraweeh and read more of it than we normally do. But let us ask ourselves how much we reflect on what Allahﷻ said to us, how much we take away, how much it changes us as it has the power to do. How tragic if we approach the Qur'an and get nothing more than the sound of its recitation and sometimes not even that? Allahﷻ said:

أَفَلَا يَتَدَبَّرُونَ الْقُرْآنَ أَمْ عَلَى قُلُوبٍ أَقْفَالُهَا

Muhammad 47: 24. *Do they not then reflect (think deeply) on the Qur'an, or are their hearts locked up (from understanding it)?*

But what is the Qur'an? My brothers and sisters, 14 centuries ago a window opened in the heavens and God spoke to man – Allahﷻ began the revelation of His Message to His Messengerﷺ. This revelation continued for 23 years from that day and ended when Rasoolullahﷺ passed away, never to be resumed until the end of time. It was not the first time that this had happened but it was to be the last. So it contained information which was not only new but which was also what humanity would need to live, prosper and flourish as long as the earth exists. It also contained in it information which no amount of scientific development can ever bring us, information about a world whose existence mankind always suspected but could never know for sure. A world that they saw everyone going to but nobody returning from to tell others what there was. A world we enter through a door called death. An entry that we have no control over but which we know we have to make.

The Qur'an not only told us about that but about what would happen to us thereafter and how we could control that at will. How we could choose the ending we want.

The Qur'an is the actual speech of Allahﷻ. It is not the meaning of what He said. It is not Rasoolullahﷺ's understanding of what Allahﷻ said. It is the actual speech of Allahﷻ. But the big question is, 'Are we listening?' Listening is different from hearing because listening is the result of understanding, not merely registering sound. So do we understand what we hear? The Qur'an is the spoken word. It was revealed as the spoken word. Not as writing on a piece of parchment. That is why listening to it is the most powerful way of approaching it. The Qur'an enters first the heart, then the mind. First it connects the spirit, then the intellect.

First it wakes us up, then tells us what we need to hear. So let's ask if we are still asleep after listening to the Qur'an for ten days this Ramadan or if we are awake. Our hard hearts will tell us, our dry eyes will tell us, our fearless lives of disobedience will tell us, our hurtling towards our own destruction while reciting the recipe for rescue will tell us. So let us ask ourselves. For there is none so destitute as the one who looked upon a treasure but returned empty handed. Allah ﷻ said about the power of His Kalaam:

لَوْ أَنزَلْنَا هَذَا الْقُرْآنَ عَلَى جَبَلٍ لَّرَأَيْتَهُ خَاشِعًا مُّتَصَدِّعًا مِّنْ خَشْيَةِ اللَّهِ وَتِلْكَ الْأَمْثَالُ نَضْرِبُهَا لِلنَّاسِ لَعَلَّهُمْ يَتَفَكَّرُونَ

***Hashr* 59: 21.** *Had We sent down this Qur'an on a mountain, you would surely have seen it humbling itself and rending asunder by the fear of Allah. Such are the parables which We put forward to mankind that they may reflect.*

He said about its effect on the hearts of the Believers:

إِنَّمَا الْمُؤْمِنُونَ الَّذِينَ إِذَا ذُكِرَ اللَّهُ وَجِلَتْ قُلُوبُهُمْ وَإِذَا تُلِيَتْ عَلَيْهِمْ آيَاتُهُ زَادَتْهُمْ إِيمَانًا وَعَلَى رَبِّهِمْ يَتَوَكَّلُونَ

***Anfal* 8: 2.** *The believers are only those who, when Allah is mentioned, feel a fear in their hearts and when His Ayaat (this Qur'an) are recited unto them, they (Ayaat) increase their Faith; and they put their trust in their Rabb (Alone)*

Let us ask if any of this happens to us and if it doesn't then is it a matter of concern? Abu Hurairah one of the personal and favorite students of Rasoolullah who dedicated his entire life only to learning from him said, 'The dryness of the eyes is a sign of the hardness of the heart.' In another Hadith Rasoolullah said, 'Allah has made the fire of Jahannam Haraam on two kinds of eyes; the eye that weeps for the Glory and Magnificence of Allah and the eye that stays awake for the protection of the Muslims.' Let us ask if we fit. Or if our eyes weep listening to poetry, watching movies and listening to dirges but not when we listen to the Glorious and Magnificent Kalaam of Allah. Yet we find nothing strange in that! That's why Allah called the ignorant, cattle and said that they are worse than cattle.

Do we reflect on the fact that what we are listening to is the actual speech of Allahﷻ revealed to Rasoolullahﷺ - from the Creator to the Best of His Creation?

Do we reflect on the fact that what we are listening to are the exact words that were revealed to Rasoolullahﷺ and which the world heard for the very first time in his voice?

Do we reflect on the fact that this message contains information that is critical to our success in this world and the next? Are we eager to know?

Are we aware as we recite that Allahﷻ is listening to us in real time and is mentioning us by name to those who are around His Arsh? Are we overwhelmed with awe and gratitude and do we fall into Sajda in thankfulness?

Are we aware that what we are reciting in Salah is what Rasoolullahﷺ recited and the Sahaba who were witness to that revelation were listening to it in the voice of the best Qari that ever lived; because he was the one to whom it was revealed? Are we excited? Or are we those who a curse can transform but the Word of Allahﷻ leaves unmoved?

Do we reflect on the fact that this Word is the most truthful word that can ever exist, that it is protected in its exactness, in its meaning and in its application by the One Who Spoke it?

Do we reflect on the fact that this Qur'an changed a people who were despised in the world and made them into role models who were looked up to?

Do we reflect on the fact that this Qur'an transformed people and changed their destination from Jahannam to Jannah? And then do we ask, 'But what is it doing for me?'

Do we reflect on the fact that Allah ﷻ has mentioned us in the Qur'an and also mentioned what will happen to each of us depending on the qualities He mentioned? And then as is the demand of intelligence, do we search for ourselves in the Qur'an?

Do we reflect on the fact that the Qur'an is Shifaa – a cure for illness; the most serious of which is the illness of the heart called Nifaaq – hypocrisy? And then do we seek that cure before it is too late?

Do we reflect on the fact that the Qur'an teaches us how to ask Allahﷻ and then do we ask Allahﷻ as He told us to ask and see the result of our dua being accepted?

Do we reflect on the fact that Qur'an gives solace to the bereaved, comfort to the aggrieved, safety from danger, takes away our fears and anxieties? And then do we seek these things from the Qur'an before we run to anyone else for help?

Do we learn to read the Qur'an properly according to its rules and do we teach our children ourselves? Or do we hire a poor Imam for a pittance and leave it to him to teach our children while ourselves not even having the knowledge to judge if he is doing the job correctly or not?

Do we take pride in the course of study our child is doing in a worldly sense and feel no shame whatsoever that our child can't read the Qur'an properly, can't lead two Raka'at of Salah and will not be able to lead our own Salaat-ul-Janaaza when we die?

Do our children listen to us reciting the Qur'an at home or is that not a part of their memory? How many homes are there which are palaces outwardly but in reality ruins; where the walls and tapestries, chandeliers and carpets are witness to Qawwali and Ghazal parties but yearn to hear the Kalaam of Allahﷻ in vain. Truly O! People on the Day of Judgment, every brick in that wall will complain to Allahﷻ about what you forced it to witness.

How many of our homes are bereft of the sound of the Kalaam of Allahﷻ? Our voices reciting His Kalaam are not a part of the memories of our children. They will remember us for many reasons, some good, some bad, but never because they used to hear us reciting the Kalaam of Allahﷻ in the dead of the night when the world was asleep.

How many of us have children who come to us and say, 'Mummy, Baba, please make dua for me because I am in this difficulty. I know your connection with your Rabb. Please ask Him to help me.' And how many of us can then lift our hands and look up at the heavens with confidence and say, 'O! Allahﷻ, give me because I am asking.'

So how can we change this state and make our Salah a thing of great joy, rejuvenating the spirit, strengthening the heart and connecting us to the Only One who has the power to change our lives to make us winners in both worlds? We can do this by praying deliberately and not mechanically. Please reflect on the importance of the Niyyah in Salah. Why is it necessary to make the Niyyah? It is not because Allah ﷻ doesn't know what we are doing. It is so that we remind ourselves of what we are about to do and to do it deliberately, consciously, thankfully with the sense of awe and gratitude to be able to stand in the presence of Allah ﷻ.

My Brothers and Sisters, I can't possibly overemphasize the importance of connecting to Allahﷻ. The Salah is the tool to do that but sadly even in Salah our attention wanders and we have made Salah a mechanical thing to be 'performed' – Allahﷻ used the term 'establish' – but we insist on calling it 'perform'. That is why it is a performance and the Dhikr of Allahﷻ and obedience to Him is never established in our lives. So let us see how we can change it so that the Salah becomes the tool to solve all our problems in this life and an intercessor for us in our graves and on the Day of Judgment. We can only connect to Allahﷻ by responding to His Kalaam. How can we connect if we are dead to the Speech of Allahﷻ, if we don't respond? Allahﷻ mentioned the effect of His Kalaam on a mountain if it were sent down on it. Please reflect, we respond even to a curse but we don't respond to the Word of Allah ﷻ. What does that say about the state of our hearts? It is only if we reflect on the Qur'an that we can reach a state where we are responsive to Allah ﷻ.

To begin with I thought I would take as a pointer the Sura which we recite most often in every Salah and without which Salah is not complete or accepted, Sura Al-Fatiha. Let us reflect on what we say when we recite this glorious Sura, so that we can remember this when we recite it and listen to its recitation and enable ourselves to connect to Allah ﷻ.

Let us reflect on the Hadith Qudsi which Imam Muslim recorded in his Sahih. *On the authority of Abu Hurayrah ﷺ from Rasoolullah ﷺ who said:*

"Allah ﷻ had said: 'I have divided prayer between Myself and My slave into two halves, and My slave shall have what he has asked for. When the slave says: 'Al-hamdu lillahi rabbi l-alamin', Allah ﷻ says: (Hamidani Abdi) 'My slave has praised Me.' And when he says: 'Ar-rahmani r-rahim', Allah ﷻ says: (Ithna Alaiyya Abdi) 'My slave has extolled Me,' and when he says: 'Maliki yawmi d-din' Allah ﷻ says: (Majjadani Abdi) 'My slave has glorified Me'. And when he says: 'Iyyaka na budu wa iyyaka nasta een', He says: (Haadha bayni wa bayna Abdi wa li Abdi ma Sa'al) 'This is between Me and My slave and My slave shall have what he has asked for.' And when he says: 'Ihdina ssirata l- mustaqim, siratal ladhina an amta alayhim ghayril-maghdubi alayhim wa la d-dallin' He says: (Haadha li Abdi wa li Abdi ma Sa'al) 'This is for My slave and My slave shall have what he has asked for.'

It is for this reason in deference to the response of Allah ﷻ to each Ayah that Rasoolullah ﷺ used to recite this Sura Ayah by Ayah and not continuously.

Let's reflect on simply two thoughts: That Allah ﷻ is actually listening and responding in real time to us when we pray and recite Sura Al Fatiha and that Allah ﷻ used the term 'Abdi' (My Slave) when he mentioned the person who is praying. That way of address alone is enough to send the one who understands what he is doing and who reflects on this Hadith into a state of ecstatic joy that he worships a Living God who is Real and who Listens to him and Responds in such an affectionate and personal way. What more can one ask?

So let us reflect on this Surah.

بِسْمِ اللّٰهِ الرَّحْمَٰنِ الرَّحِيمِ

This is the first Ayah of the Qur'an. It is also the Sunnah to start any action with this Ayah. I want you to reflect that when we say Basmallah we are actually reciting an Ayah of the Qur'an. We are beginning that action by reciting Qur'an. Imagine the Baraka of that. Naturally the Hadith where Rasoolullahﷺ told us that Allahﷻ rewards the Believer with 10 Hasanaath for every letter of the Qur'an will also apply إن شاء الله to anyone who recites this Ayah with that consciousness hoping for reward from Allahﷻ.

Basmallah is also protection against sin because it is inconceivable that you could begin something which is Haraam with the name of

Allah ﷻ. That would be blasphemy and sacrilege and not something that any Muslim, no matter how weak his faith may be, would dream of doing. So if we make it a habit to begin all our actions with Basmallah then we can be assured that remembering Allah ﷻ will stop us from committing sin.

Then think about the meaning of this Ayah. We are saying, 'In the name of Allah ﷻ...' So when we begin in the name of Allah ﷻ we think about our connection with Him. I remind myself and you that it takes a long time to build a connection but doesn't take long to break that connection. We can see this in our own relationships and know that it takes years to build trust and to create a relationship of closeness but it takes only one incident or one word to break that relationship.

So let us ask ourselves, 'What is my connection with Allahﷻ?' Nobody can say with certainty how strong and close that connection is and we will know that only when the curtain is lifted and we meet Allahﷻ. But when we begin the name of Allahﷻ we must reflect on this and ask ourselves what we are doing to build this connection. And must do our utmost to ensure that we never do anything that is likely to strain or break that connection.

We begin in the name of Allahﷻ - who is Ar-Rahman and Ar-Raheem. I will come to the meaning of these specific attributes later because they are mentioned again in the third Ayah but here let us reflect on the Baraka of beginning in the name of Allahﷻ who chose to introduce Himself with these specific attributes of his among all the other equally magnificent ones. This is to indicate the primary relationship that Allah ﷻ has with His creatures, a relationship of Mercy – overriding Mercy and Compassion. So we need to thank Allah ﷻ for introducing Himself with these Sifaat (attributes, qualities) because if He had not done that we couldn't have made Him change His Words. The introduction is important because further interaction depends on how a person introduces himself. If a person introduces himself as a doctor you won't ask him to fix your car. Similarly if a person tells you that he is a motor mechanic you will not tell him about the pain in your heart. So reflect on the importance of Allah ﷻ introducing Himself as Ar-Rahman-ur-Raheem. It defines our relationship with Him and tells us what we can expect from Him –

His Mercy and Compassion, boundless and complete.

Compassion is not merely Mercy but something that arises out of a true understanding of the difficulties and pain of the one suffering them. For example someone who has undergone heart surgery can truly understand the anxiety of the one who is waiting to be operated. For others, it is more academic because they don't share that experience though they may well sympathize with the patient. There is a special relationship between the one who is compassionate and the one who is suffering the pain; a relationship of shared experience. Who understands our pain better than Allahﷻ although He is free from our experience but is our Creator and the creator of our experiences. So we begin the

Sura and the Qur'an and must begin all our actions with the name of Allahﷻ.

الْحَمْدُ للهِ رَبِّ الْعَالَمِينَ

All goodness starts with thankfulness. Thankfulness creates Baraka in our lives, enjoyment in our experience and appreciation for what we have. So Allahﷻ taught us to begin with praising and thanking Him. Praise is for His Glorious qualities and attributes and thanks are for His Neymaat (blessings on us).

Imam Ibn Kathir in his Tafsir records this Hadith narrated by Abdullah ibn Umar‎ؓ and collected in Ibn Majah: (A slave of Allah once said, `O Allah! Yours is the Hamd that is suitable for the grace of Your Face and the greatness of Your Supreme Authority. 'The two angels were confused as to how to write these words. They ascended to Allah and said, `O our Rabb! A slave just made a statement and we are unsure how to record it for him. 'Allah asked while having more knowledge about what His slave had said, 'What did My slave say?' They said, 'He said, `O Allah! Yours is the Hamd that is suitable for the grace of Your Face and the greatness of Your Supreme Authority. 'Allah said to them, `Write it as My slave said it, until he meets Me and then I shall reward him for it.)

As for praising Allah ﷻ, He ﷻ reminded us:

قُل لَّوْ كَانَ الْبَحْرُ مِدَادًا لِّكَلِمَاتِ رَبِّي لَنَفِدَ الْبَحْرُ قَبْلَ

أَن تَنفَدَ كَلِمَاتُ رَبِّي وَلَوْ جِئْنَا بِمِثْلِهِ مَدَدًا

***Kahf* 18: 109.** *Say (O Muhammad to mankind). "If the sea were ink for (writing) the Words of my*

Rabb, surely, the sea would be exhausted before the Words of my Rabb would be finished, even if we brought (another sea) like it for its aid."

There is no power in our language to praise Allahﷻ as He is worthy of being praised. So the best we can do is to use the words that Allahﷻ Himself used to describe His Glory and Majesty. For nobody knows Allahﷻ better than He knows Himself and nobody can describe Allahﷻ better than He can describe Himself.

اللّهُ لاَ إِلَـهَ إِلاَّ هُوَ الْحَيُّ الْقَيُّومُ لاَ تَأْخُذُهُ سِنَةٌ وَلاَ نَوْمٌ لَّهُ

مَا فِي السَّمَاوَاتِ وَمَا فِي الأَرْضِ مَن ذَا الَّذِي يَشْفَعُ

عِنْدَهُ إِلاَّ بِإِذْنِهِ يَعْلَمُ مَا بَيْنَ أَيْدِيهِمْ وَمَا خَلْفَهُمْ وَلاَ

يُحِيطُونَ بِشَيْءٍ مِّنْ عِلْمِهِ إِلاَّ بِمَا شَاء وَسِعَ كُرْسِيُّهُ

السَّمَاوَاتِ وَالأَرْضَ وَلاَ يَؤُودُهُ حِفْظُهُمَا وَهُوَ الْعَلِيُّ الْعَظِيمُ

Baqara 2: 255. *Allah! La ilaha illa Huwa (none has the right to be worshipped but He), the Ever Living, the One Who sustains and protects all that exists. Neither slumber, nor sleep overtake Him. To Him belongs whatever is in the heavens and whatever is on earth. Who is he that can intercede with Him except with His Permission? He knows what happens to them (His creatures) in this world, and what will happen to them in the Hereafter . And they will never compass anything of His Knowledge except that which He wills. His Kursi extends over the heavens and the earth, and He feels no fatigue in guarding and preserving them. And He is the Most High, the Most Great.*

هُوَ اللَّهُ الَّذِي لَا إِلَهَ إِلَّا هُوَ عَالِمُ الْغَيْبِ وَالشَّهَادَةِ هُوَ
الرَّحْمَنُ الرَّحِيمُ

هُوَ اللَّهُ الَّذِي لَا إِلَهَ إِلَّا هُوَ الْمَلِكُ الْقُدُّوسُ السَّلَامُ
الْمُؤْمِنُ الْمُهَيْمِنُ الْعَزِيزُ الْجَبَّارُ الْمُتَكَبِّرُ سُبْحَانَ اللَّهِ عَمَّا
يُشْرِكُونَ

هُوَ اللَّهُ الْخَالِقُ الْبَارِئُ الْمُصَوِّرُ لَهُ الْأَسْمَاءُ الْحُسْنَى يُسَبِّحُ
لَهُ مَا فِي السَّمَاوَاتِ وَالْأَرْضِ وَهُوَ الْعَزِيزُ الْحَكِيمُ

Hashr 59: 22. *He is Allah, than Whom there is La ilaha illa Huwa (none has the right to be worshipped but He) the All-Knower of the unseen and the seen (open). He is the Most Beneficent, the Most Merciful.* **23.** *He is Allah than Whom there* *is La ilaha illa Huwa (none has the right to be worshipped but He) the King, the Holy, the One Free from all defects, the Giver of security, the Watcher over His creatures, the All-Mighty, the Compeller, the Supreme. Glory be to Allah! (High is He) above all that they associate as partners with Him.* **24.** *He is Allah, the Creator, the Inventor of all things, the Bestower of forms. To Him belong the Best Names . All that is in the heavens and the earth glorify Him. And He is the All-Mighty, the All-Wise.*

قُلْ هُوَ اللَّهُ أَحَدٌ

اللَّهُ الصَّمَدُ

لَمْ يَلِدْ وَلَمْ يُولَدْ

وَلَمْ يَكُن لَّهُ كُفُوًا أَحَدٌ

Ikhlaas 112: 1. *Say (O Muhammad): "He is Allah, (the) One.* ***2.*** *"Allah-us-Samad (The Self-Sufficient Master, Whom all creatures need).* ***3.*** *"He begets not, nor was He begotten;* ***4.****"And there is none co-equal or comparable unto Him."*

My brothers and sisters let us reflect on who we worship. We don't worship the creations of our own imagination. We don't worship celestial bodies, animals, trees, mountains, rivers or anything in creation. We worship the Only One who is worthy of being worshipped. We worship the Creator of them all and of all that we know and all that we don't know. By that we are exalted above all creation and all creation has been subjugated to us – only because we worship nothing but the Creator.

Now let us see what we need to thank Allahﷻ for. He reminded us and said:

الَّذِي أَحْسَنَ كُلَّ شَيْءٍ خَلَقَهُ وَبَدَأَ خَلْقَ الْإِنسَانِ مِن طِينٍ

ثُمَّ جَعَلَ نَسْلَهُ مِن سُلَالَةٍ مِّن مَّاءٍ مَّهِينٍ

ثُمَّ سَوَّاهُ وَنَفَخَ فِيهِ مِن رُّوحِهِ وَجَعَلَ لَكُمُ السَّمْعَ وَالْأَبْصَارَ وَالْأَفْئِدَةَ قَلِيلًا مَّا تَشْكُرُونَ

***Sajda* 32: 7.** *Who made everything He has created good, and He began the creation of man from clay.* **8.** *Then He made his offspring from semen of worthless water (male and female sexual discharge).* **9.** *Then He fashioned him in due proportion, and breathed into him the soul (created by Allah for that* *person), and He gave you hearing (ears), sight (eyes) and hearts. Little is the thanks you give!*

أَلَمْ نَجْعَلِ الْأَرْضَ مِهَادًا

وَالْجِبَالَ أَوْتَادًا

وَخَلَقْنَاكُمْ أَزْوَاجًا

وَجَعَلْنَا نَوْمَكُمْ سُبَاتًا

وَجَعَلْنَا اللَّيْلَ لِبَاسًا

وَجَعَلْنَا النَّهَارَ مَعَاشًا

وَبَنَيْنَا فَوْقَكُمْ سَبْعًا شِدَادًا

وَجَعَلْنَا سِرَاجًا وَهَّاجًا

وَأَنزَلْنَا مِنَ الْمُعْصِرَاتِ مَاء ثَجَّاجًا

لِنُخْرِجَ بِهِ حَبًّا وَنَبَاتًا

وَجَنَّاتٍ أَلْفَافًا

Naba 78: 6. *Have We not made the earth as a bed,* **7.** *And the mountains as pegs?* **8.** *And We have created you in pairs* **9.** *And have made your sleep as a thing for rest.* **10.** *And have made the night as a covering (through its darkness),* **11.** *And have made the day for livelihood.* **12.** *And We have built above you seven strong (heavens),* **13.** *And have made (therein) a shining lamp (sun).* **14.** *And have sent down from the rainy clouds abundant water.*

15. *That We may produce therewith corn and vegetation,* ***16.*** *And gardens of thick growth.*

There are many other Ayaat where Allah ﷻ reminded us of His favors. But why do we need a reminder when we look in the mirror every day? Why do we need a reminder when we walk without pain, eat without worrying about digestion, sleep without trouble and wake up feeling fresh and energetic? Why do we need a reminder when we can admire a sunrise or a sunset or a glowing florescent sunbird flitting from flower to flower, drinking nectar? Why do we need a reminder when we look at our children, parents and spouses who Allah ﷻ gave us without asking? Why do we need a reminder when we look at all those who were not as blessed as we have been at least materially? Why do we need a reminder when we stand in Salah in the presence of the Creator Himself? Why do we need a reminder except because we don't reflect? So let us reflect and make a list of all that we have to thank Allahﷻ for. **(Rabbi lakal hamdu kama yambaghi jalaali wajhika wa azeemi sultaanik)**

The best thing about thankfulness is that it enhances appreciation of what we have and that is the secret of happiness – to appreciate what we have, not hanker for what we don't have. So let us make that list before we sleep today. Don't miss out anything. For example don't miss out the fact that your beautiful, glossy flowing hair is dead tissue. If it wasn't you would need to go under anesthesia for every haircut. Let us thank Allahﷻ for all that He gave us without asking and all that He gave us when we asked for it and for all that He didn't give us even though we asked for it very much. Sometimes I believe that we need to thank Allahﷻ even more for what He didn't give us even when we asked because He knew that was not something which would benefit us. I am old enough to remember some of my duas which today I thank Allahﷻ that He didn't grant me. Truly Allahﷻ knows and we don't know.

Allahﷻ also mentioned His quality of Ruboobiyat when he referred to himself as Rabbul-A'alameen. This is the quality of Allahﷻ where He takes something incomplete stage by stage to a state of completion. Allahﷻ does that with everything in His creation, whether or not they worship Him. And that is the reason it is necessary for everyone who benefits from Allah ﷻ's Ruboobiyat to acknowledge it and to worship Him alone and not join partners with Him. Worshipping others than Allah ﷻ or joining partners with Him in his worship or in asking for help is a sign of the most despicable ingratitude for how can you take something from someone and then thank someone else who had nothing to do with what you received?

الرَّحْمٰنِ الرَّحِيمِ

Allah ﷻ mentioned His two qualities of Mercy. One of them is His personal name – Ar-Rahman – which like Allah ﷻ can't be used for anyone other than Him. It is essential to use the prefix Abd – Abdur Rahman – like we use the same prefix when we say Abdullah.

Rahman is on the same meter (Wazn) as Atshaan (extremely thirsty), Ghadhbaan (very angry), Jauaan (very hungry) – and indicates a state of the peak of Mercy. Rahman is the Merciful when He is at the peak of His Mercy. However the issue with any peak is that after that is a decline. The state of the peak doesn't last forever. And so Allah ﷻ used another of His Glorious Attributes and Qualities – Ar-Raheem. This is on the same meter (Wazn) as

Jameel (beautiful), Kareem (noble) and indicates a state which is intrinsic to someone and lasts as long as the person lives. Someone beautiful doesn't suddenly become ugly. Someone noble doesn't become ignoble. In the case of Allah ﷻ, Ar-Raheem after Ar-Rahman indicates His Mercy which is always at its peak, never faltering, never running out, never receding. We ask Allah ﷻ to cover us with His Mercy in both worlds.

My brothers and sisters, please reflect on the Mercy of Allah ﷻ that all that is essential in life, Allah ﷻ give us without charge, free. Air, water (except where we polluted is so much that we have to pay to purify it), instincts, intelligence and most importantly guidance. The Qur'an is free. It is free for anyone who is interested in listening to it, understanding it and living by it.

But please reflect that it was not free for those who received it first. Rasoolullahﷺ himself paid a personal price for the revelation. There are innumerable Ahadith which describe the enormous strain that he underwent when Allahﷻ revealed His Kalaam to him. On one occasion he was lying down with his head in the lap of one of his companions (Abdullah ibn Masaoud?) when he received Wahi. His companion said, the weight on my leg was such that I thought my leg would break. On another occasion he was riding on his camel when Wahi came and the camel was forced to its knees and knelt down because she couldn't bear the load. When Allahﷻ revealed the Ayaat about the innocence of Ayesha (RA) she narrates that it was a very cold evening but Rasoolullahﷺ had moisture dripping from his forehead to such an extent that it appeared as if he'd had a bath.

The Sahaba all paid a personal price in money, danger, lives and loss of property to receive and live by the Qur'an. They paid the price for us so that today we can live by this Kalaam free from fear, free of cost. But do we? What is our excuse?

Finally the introduction sets expectations. The introduction sets the tone for the meeting. If someone introduces himself as a physician, I would not tell him about my car. If someone introduces himself as a lawyer I would not tell him about my headache unless it had two legs and a name. So what is the implication of the way Allah ﷻ introduced Himself?

Allah ﷻ has attributes and qualities out of which He mentioned 99 to us. He is not limited to these. His qualities and glorious attributes are boundless. Among the attributes He mentioned to us are His attributes of power, majesty, glory and magnificence – Jalaal wa Jabaroot wa Kamal wal Izzah. But out of them all He chose to introduce Himself with His attributes of Infinite Mercy and Compassion. Ask why?

For a person who has Imaan in the Aakhira and who has read the Qur'an and who knows something about the trials and difficulties of the Day of Judgment; for someone who is conscious of his own weakness, his sins, his disobedience of Allah ﷻ, what do you think would happen if he was to read the introduction of Allah ﷻ as: The Avenger, The

Overpoweringly Powerful, Al Qahhaar, Al Jabbar, Al Muntaqim – and then he reads - مَالِكِ يَوْمِ الدِّينِ

He would be overpowered with terror thinking of what would probably happen to him when he would have to stand before Allahﷻ on that day. But Allahﷻ in His Infinite Mercy and Compassion, in His Infinite Grace and Forgiveness set the expectations and tone for the meeting and introduced Himself as الرَّحْمنِ الرَّحِيمِ

To reassure His slaves that His Mercy is what they can look forward to. I ask you, my brothers and sisters, if Allahﷻ had not chosen to do this and had instead introduced Himself in another way, who among us would have been able to make Him change his introduction? I ask you, should we not first of all thank Allahﷻ for introducing Himself in this way, even before we read anything further? Allahﷻ is saying to us, 'O My Slaves, you will come before me on that Day but remember that you come before the One whose Mercy is greater than His Wrath; whose Mercy is what will set the expectations of that Day and the tone of that meeting.' I ask Allahﷻ for His Mercy for us all and for His Forgiveness for all our sins or commission or omission.

Then Allahﷻ mentioned the fact that He is the Owner (King) of the Day of Judgment when He said:

مَالِكِ يَوْمِ الدِّينِ

My brothers and sisters, that day will come and we will see it. I can say that with more certainty than I can say that tomorrow will come and I will see it. So what must we do to prepare for that day when we are certain both that it will be established and that we will be a part of it, witness to it and affected by it. Allahﷻ in His Infinite Mercy gave it into our hands to write our own future for that day. We can be in as much grief and pain or happiness and comfort as we wish. What must we do therefore if we want to ensure that we escape the horrors of that day and be granted the safety and comfort of the Shade of Allahﷻ's Throne on the day when there will be no shade except His Shade. Allahﷻ told us what they day will be like.

إِذَا زُلْزِلَتِ الْأَرْضُ زِلْزَالَهَا

وَأَخْرَجَتِ الْأَرْضُ أَثْقَالَهَا

وَقَالَ الْإِنسَانُ مَا لَهَا

يَوْمَئِذٍ تُحَدِّثُ أَخْبَارَهَا

بِأَنَّ رَبَّكَ أَوْحَى لَهَا

يَوْمَئِذٍ يَصْدُرُ النَّاسُ أَشْتَاتًا لِّيُرَوْا أَعْمَالَهُمْ

فَمَن يَعْمَلْ مِثْقَالَ ذَرَّةٍ خَيْرًا يَرَهُ

وَمَن يَعْمَلْ مِثْقَالَ ذَرَّةٍ شَرًّا يَرَهُ

***Zalzala* 99: 1.** *When the earth is shaken with its (final) earthquake.* **2.** *And when the earth throws out its burdens,* **3.** *And man will say: "What is the matter with it?"* **4.** *That Day it will declare its information (about all what happened over it of good or evil).* **5.** *Because your Rabb has inspired it.* **6.** *That Day mankind will proceed in scattered groups that they may be shown their deeds.* **7.** *So whosoever does good equal to the weight of an atom (or a small ant), shall see it.* **8.** *And whosoever does evil equal to the weight of an atom (or a small ant), shall see it.*

Rasoolullahﷺ mentioned in a Hadith Narrated by Anas ibn Malik رضي الله عنه:

Rasoolullahﷺ said, "Allahﷻ will gather all the people on the Day of Judgment and they will say, 'Let us request someone to intercede for us with our Rabb so that He may relieve us from this place of ours.' Then they will go to Adamعليه السلام and say, 'You are the one whom Allahﷻ created with His Own Hands, and breathed in you of His soul, and ordered the angels to prostrate to you; so please intercede for us with our Rabb.' Adamعليه السلام will reply, 'I am not fit for this undertaking, and will remember his sin, and will say, 'Go to Noohعليه السلام, the first Messenger sent by Allahﷻ'. They will go to him and he will say, 'I am not fit for this undertaking', and will remember his sin and say, 'Go to Abrahamعليه السلام whom Allahﷻ took as a Khalil. They will go to him (and request similarly). He will reply, 'I am not fit for this undertaking,' and will remember his sin and say, 'Go to Musa عليه السلام to whom Allah جل جلاله spoke directly.' They will go to Musa عليه السلام and he will say, 'I am not fit for this undertaking,' and will remember his sin and say, 'Go to Esa عليه السلام.' They will go to him, and he will say, 'I am not fit for this undertaking, go to Muhammad ﷺ as Allah جل جلاله has forgiven his past and future sins.' They will come to me and I will ask my Rabb's permission, and when I see Him, I will fall down in prostration to Him, and He will leave me in that state as long as (He) Allah جل جلاله will, and then I will be addressed. 'Raise up your head (O Muhammad)! Ask, and your request will be granted, and say, and your saying will be listened to; intercede, and your intercession will be accepted.' Then I will raise my head, and I will glorify and praise my Rabb with a saying (dua) He will teach me, and then I will intercede. Allah ﷻ will fix a limit for me (i.e., certain type of people for whom I may intercede), and I will take them out of the (Jahannam) Fire and let them enter Jannah. Then I will come back (to Allah) and fall in prostration, and will do the same for the third and fourth times till no-one remains in the (Jahannam) Fire except those whom the Qur'an has imprisoned therein." (The sub-narrator, Qatada used to say at that point, "...those upon whom eternity (Jahannam) has been imposed.") (Bukhari, Kitab-u-Riqaq, Vol. 6, Hadith # 3)

My brothers and sisters please reflect; who is this Rasool? Who is the one who will be given intercession and who we hope will intercede for us? He is the one whose Sunnah we find so difficult to follow. He is the one who we don't want to resemble in our appearance, our actions, our speech, our dealings or our way of life. If this is not the case, then please look in the mirror and look into your daily lives and find signs of the Sunnah of Muhammad ﷺ. Tell me, is it loyalty and love to do the opposite of what he used to do, what he ordered us to do but still claim to love him?

About that Day Allah ﷻ warned us and asked us a question. He said:

إِذَا السَّمَاءُ انفَطَرَتْ

وَإِذَا الْكَوَاكِبُ انتَثَرَتْ

وَإِذَا الْبِحَارُ فُجِّرَتْ

وَإِذَا الْقُبُورُ بُعْثِرَتْ

عَلِمَتْ نَفْسٌ مَّا قَدَّمَتْ وَأَخَّرَتْ

يَا أَيُّهَا الْإِنسَانُ مَا غَرَّكَ بِرَبِّكَ الْكَرِيمِ

***Infitaar 82:* 1.** *When the heaven is cleft asunder.* **2.** *And when the stars have fallen and scattered;* **3.** *And when the seas are burst forth;* **4.** *And when the graves are turned upside down (and they bring out their contents)* **5.** *(Then) a person will know what he has sent forward and (what he has) left behind.* **6.** *O man! What has made you careless concerning your Rabb, the Most Generous?*

And Allah ﷻ told us about that Day and what would happen to the world we know:

إِذَا الشَّمْسُ كُوِّرَتْ

وَإِذَا النُّجُومُ انكَدَرَتْ

وَإِذَا الْجِبَالُ سُيِّرَتْ

وَإِذَا الْعِشَارُ عُطِّلَتْ

وَإِذَا الْوُحُوشُ حُشِرَتْ

وَإِذَا الْبِحَارُ سُجِّرَتْ

وَإِذَا النُّفُوسُ زُوِّجَتْ

وَإِذَا الْمَوْؤُودَةُ سُئِلَتْ

بِأَيِّ ذَنبٍ قُتِلَتْ

وَإِذَا الصُّحُفُ نُشِرَتْ

وَإِذَا السَّمَاءُ كُشِطَتْ

وَإِذَا الْجَحِيمُ سُعِّرَتْ

وَإِذَا الْجَنَّةُ أُزْلِفَتْ

عَلِمَتْ نَفْسٌ مَّا أَحْضَرَتْ

***Takwir 81:* 1.** *When the sun Kuwwirat (wound up, lost its light, overthrown).* **2.** *And when the stars shall fall;* **3.** *And when the mountains shall made to pass away;* **4.** *And when the pregnant she-camels shall be neglected;* **5.** *And when the wild beasts shall be gathered together;* **6.** *And when the seas shall become as blazing Fire or shall overflow;* **7.** *And* *when the souls shall be joined with their bodies;* **8.** *And when the female (infant) buried alive (as the pagan Arabs used to do) shall be questioned.* **9.** *For what sin she was killed?* **10.** *And when the written pages of deeds (good and bad) of every person shall be laid open;* **11.** *And when the heaven shall be stripped off and taken away from its place;* **12.** *And when Hell-fire shall be kindled to fierce ablaze.* **13.** *And when Paradise shall be brought near,* **14.** *(Then) every person will know what he has brought (of good and evil).*

I remind myself that when I hear or read مَالِكِ يَوْمِ الدِّينِ am I thinking at least about some of these things? Allahﷻ mentioned the Day of Judgment in such detail in the Qur'an that especially the last Juz is full of these descriptions. But do we reflect? Reflection is a function of importance – we reflect only on those things we consider important. So if we don't reflect on the Day of Judgment then we should ask, 'Why?' Is it that we don't think it will happen to us? Why then don't we reflect?

And Allah ﷻ told us about His Own Glory which will be visible on that day:

يَوْمَ يَقُومُ الرُّوحُ وَالْمَلَائِكَةُ صَفًّا لَّا يَتَكَلَّمُونَ إِلَّا مَنْ أَذِنَ لَهُ الرَّحْمَٰنُ وَقَالَ صَوَابًا

ذَٰلِكَ الْيَوْمُ الْحَقُّ فَمَن شَاءَ اتَّخَذَ إِلَىٰ رَبِّهِ مَآبًا

Naba 78: 38. *The Day that Ar-Ruh [Jibrael (Gabriel) or another angel] and the angels will stand forth in rows, none shall speak except him*

whom the Most Beneficent (Allah) allows, and he will speak what is right. **39.** *That is without doubt the True Day, so, whosoever wills, let him seek a place with (or a way to) His Rabb (by obeying Him in this worldly life)!*

Allah ﷻ told us about what will happen to the Believers and the Deniers on that Day.

يَوْمَ تَرَى الْمُؤْمِنِينَ وَالْمُؤْمِنَاتِ يَسْعَى نُورُهُم بَيْنَ أَيْدِيهِمْ وَبِأَيْمَانِهِم بُشْرَاكُمُ الْيَوْمَ جَنَّاتٌ تَجْرِي مِن تَحْتِهَا الْأَنْهَارُ خَالِدِينَ فِيهَا ذَٰلِكَ هُوَ الْفَوْزُ الْعَظِيمُ

يَوْمَ يَقُولُ الْمُنَافِقُونَ وَالْمُنَافِقَاتُ لِلَّذِينَ آمَنُوا انظُرُونَا نَقْتَبِسْ مِن نُّورِكُمْ قِيلَ ارْجِعُوا وَرَاءَكُمْ فَالْتَمِسُوا نُورًا

فَضُرِبَ بَيْنَهُم بِسُورٍ لَّهُ بَابٌ بَاطِنُهُ فِيهِ الرَّحْمَةُ وَظَاهِرُهُ مِن

قِبَلِهِ الْعَذَابُ

يُنَادُونَهُمْ أَلَمْ نَكُن مَّعَكُمْ قَالُوا بَلَى وَلَكِنَّكُمْ فَتَنتُمْ

أَنفُسَكُمْ وَتَرَبَّصْتُمْ وَارْتَبْتُمْ وَغَرَّتْكُمُ الْأَمَانِيُّ حَتَّى جَاء أَمْرُ

اللَّهِ وَغَرَّكُم بِاللَّهِ الْغَرُورُ

فَالْيَوْمَ لَا يُؤْخَذُ مِنكُمْ فِدْيَةٌ وَلَا مِنَ الَّذِينَ كَفَرُوا مَأْوَاكُمُ

النَّارُ هِيَ مَوْلَاكُمْ وَبِئْسَ الْمَصِيرُ

أَلَمْ يَأْنِ لِلَّذِينَ آمَنُوا أَن تَخْشَعَ قُلُوبُهُمْ لِذِكْرِ اللَّهِ وَمَا نَزَلَ

مِنَ الْحَقِّ وَلَا يَكُونُوا كَالَّذِينَ أُوتُوا الْكِتَابَ مِن قَبْلُ فَطَالَ

عَلَيْهِمُ الْأَمَدُ فَقَسَتْ قُلُوبُهُمْ وَكَثِيرٌ مِّنْهُمْ فَاسِقُونَ

Hadeed 57: 12. *On the Day you shall see the believing men and the believing women their light running forward before them and by their right hands. Glad tidings for you this Day! Gardens under which rivers flow, to dwell therein forever! Truly, this is the great success!*

13. *On the Day when the hypocrites men and women will say to the believers: "Wait for us! Let us get something from your light!" It will be said: "Go back to your rear! Then seek a light!" So a wall will be put up between them, with a gate therein. Inside it will be mercy, and outside it will be torment."*

14. *(The hypocrites) will call the believers: "Were we not with you?" The believers will reply: "Yes! But you led yourselves into temptations, you looked forward for our destruction; you doubted (in Faith);*

and you were deceived by false desires, till the Command of Allah came to pass. And the chief deceiver (Satan) deceived you in respect of Allah."

15. *So this Day no ransom shall be taken from you (hypocrites), nor of those who disbelieved, (Kuffar). Your abode is the Fire, that is the proper place for you, and worst indeed is that destination.*

16. *Has not the time come for the hearts of those who believe (in Islam) to be affected by Allah's Reminder (this Qur'an), and that which has been revealed of the truth, lest they become as those who received the Scripture [Taurat and Injeel] before (i.e. Jews and Christians), and the term was prolonged for them and so their hearts were hardened? And many of them were Fasiqun (rebellious).*

Now one thing that I want to draw to your attention as we think about all this; reflect on the Ayah before this one by which Allah ﷻ chose to introduce Himself before he mentioned the Day of Judgment - الرَّحْمَٰنِ الرَّحِيمِ

What if He had chosen to introduce Himself by the attributes he described Himself with in another place where He said:

يَوْمَ هُم بَارِزُونَ لَا يَخْفَىٰ عَلَى اللَّهِ مِنْهُمْ شَيْءٌ لِّمَنِ الْمُلْكُ الْيَوْمَ لِلَّهِ الْوَاحِدِ الْقَهَّارِ

Ghafir 40: 16. *The Day when they will (all) come out, nothing of them will be hidden from Allah. Whose is the kingdom this Day? (Allah Himself will reply to His Question): It is Allah's the One, the Irresistible!*

What would be the state of being of the true believer when he reflected on the Jalaal (Magnificence, Awe, Majesty, Glory, Power) of Allah ﷻ and then thought of facing Him on the Day of Judgment with his own life and deeds to answer for?

What do you say about the Rabb, who is Al Waahidul Qahhaar, Al Jabbar ul Muntaqim, Al Aziz ul Hakeem – but when He first spoke about the Day of Judgment, he introduced Himself as Ar-Rahman ur Raheem?

What do you say to the Rabb who is saying, 'O! My slave, you will face me on that day but don't worry, I am Ar-Rahman ur Raheem. There is nobody who is more merciful and compassionate than I am.' That is why we need to reflect so that we can build a connection with Allah ﷻ.

Rasoolullah ﷺ said: "Allah has divided mercy into 100 parts, and He retained with Him 99 parts, and sent down to earth 1 part. Through this one part creatures deal with one another with compassion, so much so that an animal lifts its hoof over its young lest it should hurt it." (Al-Bukhari)

Rasoolullah ﷺ also said, "Those who show mercy to their fellow beings will be shown mercy by the Merciful Rabb. So, show mercy to those on the earth, and He Who is in the heaven will show mercy to you." (At-Tirmidhi)

And he said, "Allah ordered the appointed angels over you that the good and the bad deeds be written, and He then showed how to write. If someone intends to do a good deed and he does not do it, then Allah will write for him a full good deed, and if he intends to do a good deed and actually did it, then Allah will write for him its reward equal from 10 to 700 times to many more times. And If someone intends to do a bad deed and he does not do it, then Allah will write for him a full good deed (in his account) with Him, and if he intends to do a bad deed and actually did it, then Allah will write for him one bad deed." (Al-Bukhari)

Rasoolullahﷺ said, "Allah, the Almighty, says, 'Whosoever does a good deed, will have a reward 10 times like it and I add more, and whosoever does an evil, will have the punishment like it or I will forgive him, and whosoever approaches Me by one span, I will approach him by one cubit, and whosoever approaches Me by one cubit, I approach him by one fathom, and whosoever comes to Me walking, I go to him running, and whosoever meets Me with an earth-load of sins without associating anything with Me, I meet him with forgiveness like that." (Muslim)

Allahﷻ reminded us, His slaves that He is ready to forgive any sin provided we are ready to repent. So let us make haste in our repentance because the time for it is only until we see the angels. Delaying in repentance is a sign of weakness of Imaan. Allahﷻ reassured those who want to repent but are afraid about their past and are ashamed to go before Allahﷻ as they are not sure if He will forgive them. Remember that this fear is a sign of Imaan and a very welcome one at that.

قُلْ يَا عِبَادِيَ الَّذِينَ أَسْرَفُوا عَلَى أَنفُسِهِمْ لَا تَقْنَطُوا مِن رَّحْمَةِ اللَّهِ إِنَّ اللَّهَ يَغْفِرُ الذُّنُوبَ جَمِيعًا إِنَّهُ هُوَ الْغَفُورُ الرَّحِيمُ

***Zumar* 39: 53.** *Say: "O 'Ibadi (My slaves) who have transgressed against themselves (by committing evil deeds and sins)! Despair not of the Mercy of Allah, verily Allah forgives all sins. Truly, He is Oft-Forgiving, Most Merciful.*

As they say, 'Every pious person has a past and every sinner has a future.'

And then, as if this was not enough, Allah ﷻ in His infinite Mercy said this:

إِلَّا مَن تَابَ وَآمَنَ وَعَمِلَ عَمَلًا صَالِحًا فَأُوْلَئِكَ يُبَدِّلُ اللَّهُ

سَيِّئَاتِهِمْ حَسَنَاتٍ وَكَانَ اللَّهُ غَفُورًا رَّحِيمًا

Al Furqaan 25: 70. *Except those who repent and believe (in Islam), and do righteous deeds, for those, Allah will change their sins into good deeds, and Allah is Oft-Forgiving, Most Merciful.*

Now what do we say about a Rabb who not only promised to forgive but promised to convert sins into good deeds for the one who repents? Truly the Mercy of Allah ﷻ is beyond our understanding.

Then finally Allah ﷻ taught us to make dua and said:

لاَ يُكَلِّفُ اللهُ نَفْسًا إِلاَّ وُسْعَهَا لَهَا مَا كَسَبَتْ وَعَلَيْهَا مَا

اكْتَسَبَتْ رَبَّنَا لاَ تُؤَاخِذْنَا إِن نَّسِينَا أَوْ أَخْطَأْنَا رَبَّنَا وَلاَ

تَحْمِلْ عَلَيْنَا إِصْرًا كَمَا حَمَلْتَهُ عَلَى الَّذِينَ مِن قَبْلِنَا رَبَّنَا وَلاَ

تُحَمِّلْنَا مَا لاَ طَاقَةَ لَنَا بِهِ وَاعْفُ عَنَّا وَاغْفِرْ لَنَا وَارْحَمْنَآ

أَنتَ مَوْلاَنَا فَانصُرْنَا عَلَى الْقَوْمِ الْكَافِرِينَ

Baqara 2:286. *Allah burdens not a person beyond his scope. He gets reward for that (good) which he has earned, and he is punished for that (evil) which he has earned. "Our Rabb! Punish us not if we forget or fall into error, our Rabb! Lay not on us a burden like that which You did lay on those before us; our Rabb! Put not on us a burden greater than we have strength to bear. Pardon us and grant us Forgiveness. Have mercy on us. You are* *our Maula (Patron, Supporter, Protector) and give us victory over the disbelievers."*

We ask Allah ﷻ to be our Maula on the Day of Judgment when there will be no helpers except Him and we ask Him to be pleased with us and to enable us to please Him.

إِيَّاكَ نَعْبُدُ وإِيَّاكَ نَسْتَعِينُ

This Ayah is the essence of Tawhid ul Uloohiya and Tawhid ur Ruboobiya. If someone asks you to describe the Islamic Aqeeda in one line, you couldn't do better than to simply quote this one Ayah – You alone we worship and You alone we ask for help. This Ayah is our Covenant with Allahﷻ as Muslims (those who have submitted to Allahﷻ) and we renew it every time we pray. We remind ourselves of what we promised to do – to worship only Allahﷻ and to ask help only from Allahﷻ.

This is our promise to Allahﷻ. How shameful and dangerous it is to renege on that promise when we complete Salah. When the slave recites or hears this Ayah he must reflect on his own belief and actions to see if they are in conformation of what he just said.

How strange that we say إِيَّاكَ نَعْبُدُ وإِيَّاكَ نَسْتَعِينُ .

and then bow before others and ask for help from others. This is the problem with Muslims falling into open and hidden Shirk of various kinds. I remind myself and you to stay away from all forms of Shirk and remember this Ayah which we recite in every Raka'at in every Salah.

What do you do when you are finally standing before the King? You are one among millions. You want to ask Him for the biggest favor in your life. You want to ask Him in a way that

He will acknowledge you and recognize you and not refuse you. So what do you do?

You first establish your relationship with Him. You tell Him who you are and how you are loyal to Him alone and therefore He should listen to you. You renew your Covenant with Him. For every Covenant is two way – you promise to do something as a result of which you get some special consideration. That is what you are doing when you are saying إِيَّاكَ

نَعْبُدُ وإِيَّاكَ نَسْتَعِينُ .

You are speaking to Him, one on one. Directly without anyone in between; not through anyone. Many people ask, 'How can we ask

Allah ﷻ directly?' They should reflect on what they do every time they say إِيَّاكَ نَعْبُدُ وإِيَّاكَ نَسْتَعِينُ

Allah ﷻ taught us to ask Him directly. إِيَّاكَ is a form of address used with someone you are standing in the presence of; someone who you are standing before; who is in front of you. It is direct, first person. You, as in, 'You! I am talking to You.' That is how close this form of communication is. You alone we worship. You alone we bow to. You alone are our Ma'abood. You alone and nobody along with you or in your place. You alone we ask for help. You alone can help us. Nobody and nothing else other than you has any power to help or harm.

You and only you can help and so we ask only You.

And that is why Allah ﷻ responds and says: 'Haadha bayni wa bayna Abdi wa li Abdi ma Sa'al – This is between Me and my slave and for my slave is whatever he asks for.' Allah ﷻ acknowledges the relationship of the Abd – the slave and says, 'This is a matter between My slave and Me. And I will give My slave what he asks for.'

My brothers and sisters let us reflect on this. What is the value of having our relationship with the Creator, Ruler, Sustainer and Rabb of the Heavens and the Earth acknowledged by Himself? What is the value of Him responding by saying, 'I will give him whatever he asks of me.' It is this relationship that we have to work on and build so that we are recognized on its basis. The relationship of the Rabb with his Abd is the closest of relationships that exist. It is the only relationship that lasts long after all worldly relationships are over. It is the only relationship that will continue to benefit us in the place which really matters, the Day of Judgment. There is no relationship that is closer or more superior to that. Anyone who compromises that relationship for the sake of a relationship with any creature is a truly foolish and ignorant person.

It is about this relationship that Rasoolullahﷺ mentioned:

Narrated Safwan bin Muhriz Al-Mazini: While I was walking with Ibn `Umar holding his hand, a man came in front of us and asked,

"What have you heard from Rasoolullahﷺ about An-Najwa?" Ibn `Umar said, "I heard Rasoolullahﷺ saying, 'Allahﷻ will bring a believer near Him and shelter him with His Screen and ask him: Did you commit such-and-such sins? He will say: Yes, my Rabb. Allahﷻ will keep on asking him till he will confess all his sins and will think that he is ruined. Allahﷻ will say: 'I did screen your sins in the world and I forgive them for you today', and then he will be given the book of his good deeds. Regarding infidels and hypocrites (their evil acts will be exposed publicly) and the witnesses will say: These are the people who lied against their Rabb. Behold! The Curse of Allah is upon the wrongdoers." (11.18) Sahih al-Bukhari 2441

Ask yourself what this relationship is worth to you and then ask if it is worth ruining for the sake of your friends and relatives who insist on displeasing and angering Allah ﷻ. Please reflect that the major reason why otherwise good Muslims fall into Haraam is to please their friends. That is the reason why it is critical to keep good company. In the company of people who are obedient to Allah ﷻ it will be difficult to be disobedient to Him. In the company of people who play games with Allah ﷻ it is difficult to go against the flow especially for those who lack self-confidence and seek acceptance in society. They are ready to bend over backwards to please their friends and 'make it' into their circle, even at the risk of displeasing Allah ﷻ. This is a sign of weak

Imaan in the Aakhira and a major danger signal.

That is why Ibn Al Qayyim said, 'Sura Al-Fatiha is Tawba.' When the slave reads each Ayah he reflects on his own life and makes Tawba. What's the effect of doing that a minimum of five times a day? Or to put it more accurately, 17 times a day – 17 Raka'at of Fardh Salah. Add the Sunnah to it and you have 12 more. A Muslim renews his covenant with Allah ﷻ 29 times a day. What more is needed?

So now that the slave has the attention of Allah ﷻ and this wonderful response – Ask and it will be given – what does he ask for? What is he taught to ask for? Before we go the Ayah let us reflect on what we would like to ask if there was only one thing that we could ask for. Naturally you would like to ask for that one fundamental thing which would guarantee everything else without being asked for.

I am reminded of a short teaching story in this context. It is said that there was a man who was very poor, had no children and had a mother who was blind. One day an angel appeared to him and said, 'Ask me one thing and I will give it to you. But you can ask for only one thing.' The man said to him, 'I wish that my mother could see her grandchildren playing with toys of gold.' In that one wish he covered all his needs. So if we were to ask Allahﷻ for only one thing, what would we ask?

And that is what Allah ﷻ taught us to ask for:

اهدِنَــا الصِّرَاطَ المستَقِيمَ

Siraatal Mustaqeem – the Path of Steadfastness, the Path of Guidance, the Path of Righteousness. The one path that ensures success in this world and the next. Please reflect on the benefits of being steadfast and righteous in this life. That is the ticket to success in this world. The ticket to popularity, honor, respect and influence. If you are righteous and steadfast – integrity and consistency – you can't possibly go wrong. Read the biographies of all great leaders. I am not talking about flash in the pan political scamsters who come and go. I am talking about great leaders from any country or culture that the world talks about with great respect and you will find these two qualities in them – integrity and consistency. That is Siraatal Mustaqeem in this Dunya. The Islamic Siraatal Mustaqeem which Allahﷻ taught us to ask Him for takes this into its ambit and adds the critical aspect of the Aakhira. That's what makes this idea so powerful. It is the route to success in both worlds.

So what is Siratul Mustaqeem? What are we asking for when we ask Allahﷻ to guide us to Siratul Mustaqeem? Allahﷻ mentioned Siratul Mustaqeem in His Kalaam when He said about His Messengerﷺ:

يس

وَالْقُرْآنِ الْحَكِيمِ

إِنَّكَ لَمِنَ الْمُرْسَلِينَ

عَلَىٰ صِرَاطٍ مُّسْتَقِيمٍ

1. *Ya-Sin.* **2.** *By the Qur'an, full of wisdom (i.e. full of laws, evidences, and proofs),* **3.** *Truly, you (O Muhammad) are one of the Messengers,* **4.** *On a Straight Path (i.e. on Allah's religion of Islamic Monotheism).*

Siratul Mustaqeem is the path of the Anbiya of Allahﷻ. The path of Rasoolullahﷺ who Allahﷻ specifically mentioned and certified that he was on the Siratul Mustaqeem. And that is what we are asking Allahﷻ when we say اهدِنَا الصِّرَاطَ المستَقِيمَ

We are asking Allah ﷻ to guide us to the path of Rasoolullah ﷺ; to the Sunnah of Muhammad ﷺ; to his way of life in its entirety. Please note, we are not asking to be guided only to the way he used to pray or his charity but to his entire way of life.

My brothers and sisters, Islam is a practice. It is a Deen. A way of life. It is not an ideology. It is not some theory or philosophy to be studied, debated, discussed and then forgotten while we lead our lives any way we please. Islam is Siratul Mustaqeem. Islam is the Sunnah because the Sunnah is the living demonstration of Islam. Rasoolullah ﷺ was the living Qur'an. That is why Allah ﷻ sent him – to show how, to those who know why.

When we ask Allah ﷻ for guidance and say اهدِنَـا الصِّرَاطَ المُستَقِيم let us reflect on what our own attitude is towards the Sunnah. Sura Al-Fatiha is Tawba and so let us make Tawba for neglecting and may Allah ﷻ forgive us, deliberately ignoring and going against the Sunnah. Let us make the Niyyah to stop this forthwith and to start following the Sunnah to the best of our ability. Let us realise the master plan of those who want to hurt Islam. They know they can't tamper with the Qur'an, so what they have done is to devalue the importance of Hadith and Sunnah in the eyes of the Ummah. They tried to divorce the theory from the practice. They tried to separate the word from the action so that we would never benefit from the word.

Sadly our mentally challenged members bought into that argument and failed to see the diabolical plan behind the screen – to destroy the foundation of Islam and reduce it from a complete, practical way of life to at best, a nice theory. Islam came to change the world and has the power to do that. The Sahaba showed us this in practice. Yet today we refuse to accept the advantages of what we have and run around scared of I don't know what. The world respects whatever you do with confidence. What's so bad about the Sunnah that you don't want to practice it? Please ask yourself these questions seriously and make changes in your life.

My brothers and sisters, the Sunnah is Islam and the Sunnah is Fardh. It has not been left to our own whims and fancies to practice or leave the Sunnah. Allahﷻ put great Baraka in following the Sunnah and warned those who refuse to practice it. He said:

قُلْ إِن كُنتُمْ تُحِبُّونَ اللَّهَ فَاتَّبِعُونِي يُحْبِبْكُمُ اللَّهُ وَيَغْفِرْ لَكُمْ
ذُنُوبَكُمْ وَاللَّهُ غَفُورٌ رَّحِيمٌ

A'al Imran 3: 31. *Say (O Muhammad to mankind): "If you (really) love Allah then follow me (make my Ittiba – imitate me), Allah will love you and forgive you your sins. And Allah is Oft-Forgiving, Most Merciful."*

Ask yourself, 'Do I want Allahﷻ to love me?' Ask yourself, 'What is the benefit of having Allahﷻ love me? Is there a benefit for me if Allahﷻ loves me?' Seriously ask yourself these apparently obvious questions. From our lives it doesn't appear that they are obvious, because if they were, how is it that we don't follow the Sunnah? So let us get serious and ask if we want Allah ﷻ to love us; if we want Allah ﷻ to forgive our sins. To accept our dua and help and protect us. Then reflect on the fact that it is so easy to ensure this. Just follow the Sunnah of Rasoolullah ﷺ.

How wonderful that to do this is so full of grace and dignity; so full of goodness all around. It is not something that is difficult to do. It is easy and beneficial in this world and earns Allah ﷻ's pleasure and you become the beloved of Allah ﷻ - you become a Wali of Allah ﷻ. What more can one ask? Don't you want your dua to be accepted? Don't you want the angels to recognize you as an Ummati of

Muhammadﷺ? What is the value of being recognized as an Ummati of Muhammadﷺ?

Allahﷻ also warned those who are engrossed in the Dunya and for whom the approval of every loser is more important than the approval of Allahﷻ. He said:

قُلْ إِن كَانَ آبَاؤُكُمْ وَأَبْنَآؤُكُمْ وَإِخْوَانُكُمْ وَأَزْوَاجُكُمْ وَعَشِيرَتُكُمْ وَأَمْوَالٌ اقْتَرَفْتُمُوهَا وَتِجَارَةٌ تَخْشَوْنَ كَسَادَهَا وَمَسَاكِنُ تَرْضَوْنَهَا أَحَبَّ إِلَيْكُم مِّنَ اللّهِ وَرَسُولِهِ وَجِهَادٍ فِي سَبِيلِهِ فَتَرَبَّصُواْ حَتَّى يَأْتِيَ اللّهُ بِأَمْرِهِ وَاللّهُ لاَ يَهْدِي الْقَوْمَ الْفَاسِقِينَ

***Tawba* 9: 24.** *Say: If your fathers, your sons, your brothers, your wives, your kindred, the wealth that* *you have gained, the commerce in which you fear a decline, and the dwellings in which you delight ... are dearer to you than Allah and His Messenger, and striving hard and fighting in His Cause , then wait until Allah brings about His Decision (punishment). And Allah guides not the people who are Al-Fasiqun (rebellious, disobedient to Allah).*

Allah ﷻ enumerated all those things we love in this life and all those whose opinions we value and whose approval we seek and said clearly that if we don't love Allah ﷻ, His Messenger ﷺ and struggle in His path more than all of them, then He would reject us and punish us. What is the sign of love for Allah ﷻ? To follow the Sunnah of Muhammad ﷺ. What is the sign of love of Rasoolullah ﷺ? To follow the Sunnah of Rasoolullah ﷺ. And the struggle in this path is a source of great blessing. When will we realise the value of this, O! People? When will we realise the value of this? Why do we deliberately refuse to accept the Mercy of Allah ﷻ? Why do we refuse to accept the honor of the Sunnah of Rasoolullah ﷺ? Yet we ask Allah ﷻ to guide us to the Sunnah in every Raka'at of every Salah. Isn't that strange? Why do we lie?

The Messenger ﷺ said, 'Some people will come on the Day of Judgment and their Imaan will be outstanding, it's light will shine from their chests and from their right hands. It will be said to them, 'Glad tidings to you today. As salaamu alaikum and goodness for you; enter into it (Jannah) forever. The angels and Prophets will be jealous of the love Allah ﷻ has for them.

The Sahaba asked, 'Who are they Ya Rasoolullahﷺ?' He replied, 'They are not from you. You are my companions but they are my beloved. They will come after you and will find the Book (Qur'an) made redundant by the people and a Sunnah which has been killed by them. So they will grab hold of the Book and the Sunnah and will revive them.

They will read them and teach them (Qur'an and Sunnah) to the people and they will experience in that path a punishment (trails) more severe and more ugly than what you (Sahaba) have experienced. Indeed the Imaan of one of them is equivalent to the Imaan of forty of you. The Shaheed of one of them is equivalent to forty of your Shuhadaa. Because you found a helper towards the truth (Rasoolullahﷺ) but they will find no helper towards the truth. They will be surrounded by tyrant rulers in every place. They will be in the surroundings of Bayt ul-Maqdis (Al Quds). The Nusrah of Allah ﷻ will come to them and they will have the honor of it on their hands." Then he ﷺ said, 'O Allah ﷻ give them Nusrah and make them my close friends in Jannah." (Musnad Ahmad # 17561. Chain # 77. Hasan according to Ibn Hajr al-Haythami)

My brothers and sisters, stick to the Sunnah and reject all innovations, all Bida'at. In that there is Khair for us. Remember that you asked Allah ﷻ for this in Salah. How can you then reject what you asked for? Make Tawba and change your ways lest you be held among those who said one thing and did something else. People who angered Allah ﷻ to the extent where He refused to forgive them even if the

Messenger ﷺ made dua for them – the Munafiqoon. May Allah ﷻ protect us from following their path.

We come to the last Ayah of this beautiful Sura where Allah ﷻ further clarified what Siratul Mustaqeem is. He said:

صِرَاطَ الَّذِينَ أَنعَمتَ عَلَيهِمْ غَيرِ المغضُوبِ عَلَيهِمْ وَلاَ الضَّالِّينَ

Please reflect: the dua for guidance effectively is over with اهدِنَـا الصِّرَاطَ المستَقِيمَ صِرَاطَ الَّذِينَ أَنعَمتَ عَلَيهِمْ غَيرِ المغضُوبِ عَلَيهِمْ وَلاَ الضَّالِّينَ is really further clarifying and reiterating what we asked for; Siratul Mustaqeem; what it is and what it is not.

So first what it is: صِرَاطَ الَّذِينَ أَنعَمتَ عَلَيهِمْ

Consider this; when you want to show someone the way to some place and want to be doubly sure that the person will not make a mistake, you say, 'Go this way and not that way.' Saying simply, 'Go this way', was sufficient. But you want to make doubly sure. So you add, 'Not that way.' And that is what Allahﷻ taught us to ask for; the way of those who received His blessings and earned His pleasure and not the way of those who incurred His anger and those who fell into misguidance. Truly the Qur'an is a Book in which there is no doubt. A Book which is completely clear for those whose hearts are pure and in whose hearts there is no disease of hypocrisy. Truly the Qur'an will be a witness for us or against us on the Day of Judgment. A Witness whose evidence we will not be able to deny or refute. A Witness who will be listened to; a Witness who will intercede for us or complain against us.

Who were those who earned Allah ﷻ's pleasure? Allah ﷻ mentioned them and said:

وَمَن يُطِعِ اللَّهَ وَالرَّسُولَ فَأُوْلَئِكَ مَعَ الَّذِينَ أَنْعَمَ اللَّهُ عَلَيْهِم مِّنَ النَّبِيِّينَ وَالصِّدِّيقِينَ وَالشُّهَدَاء وَالصَّالِحِينَ وَحَسُنَ أُولَئِكَ رَفِيقًا

Nisa 4: 69. *And whoso obeys Allah and the Messenger (Muhammad), will be in the company of those on whom Allah has bestowed His Grace, of the Prophets, the Siddiqun, the martyrs, and the righteous. And how excellent these companions are!*

Allahﷻ not only mentioned those who received His Blessing and Grace but promised to keep those who obey Allahﷻ and His Messengerﷺ with them. Ask yourself, 'Do you want to be resurrected with Rasoolullahﷺ?' Then follow his Sunnah.

Allahﷻ also mentioned this matter of following the Sunnah and the reward for it in Sura Tawba:

وَالسَّابِقُونَ الأَوَّلُونَ مِنَ الْمُهَاجِرِينَ وَالأَنصَارِ وَالَّذِينَ اتَّبَعُوهُم بِإِحْسَانٍ رَّضِيَ اللهُ عَنْهُمْ وَرَضُواْ عَنْهُ وَأَعَدَّ لَهُمْ جَنَّاتٍ تَجْرِي تَحْتَهَا الأَنْهَارُ خَالِدِينَ فِيهَا أَبَدًا ذَلِكَ الْفَوْزُ الْعَظِيمُ

***Tawba* 9: 100.** *And the first to embrace Islam of the Muhajirun and the Ansar and also those who followed them exactly (in Faith). Allah is well-pleased with them as they are well-pleased with Him. He has prepared for them Gardens under which rivers flow (Paradise), to dwell therein forever. That is the supreme success.*

When the slave recites this last Ayah of Sura Al-Fatiha he reflects on what he is asking Allah ﷻ for and what he needs to do for his dua to be answered. He makes Tawba and changes his ways to follow the Sunnah of Rasoolullah ﷺ which he asked Allah ﷻ for.

Then as I said, you want to make doubly sure that the person doesn't take the wrong path, so you say, 'Not that way.' غَيرِ المغضُوبِ عَلَيهِمْ وَلاَ الضَّالِّينَ

'Not the way of those who earned your anger or the way of those who went astray.' When the slave recites this part of the Ayah he makes Tawba for all those things in his life which are likely to incur the anger of Allahﷻ and asks for Allahﷻ's forgiveness. And then he looks for all those things which are really misguidance and makes Tawba and seeks forgiveness for them.

It is true that this part of the Ayah is usually translated with the meaning of المَغضُوبِ عَلَيهِمْ as being the Jews and الضَّالِّينَ as being Christians and this is correct.

However it is incorrect to restrict the meaning to Jews and Christians. Allah ﷻ could have simply said, 'Not the way of Jews and Christians', if that was all that was meant. But he didn't and instead he gave us criteria to judge ourselves. Allah ﷻ is concerned with the actions of people. Not with who they are. So we ask protection from all things that anger Allah ﷻ and all actions of misguidance. That is why as I mentioned earlier Imam Ibn Al Qayyim Al Jawziyya said that Sura Al-Fatiha is Tawba. Reflect that Tawba cleanses us, converts our sins into good deeds and saves us from the anger and punishment of Allah ﷻ. Allah ﷻ gives us the opportunity to make Tawba every time we stand before Him. How much must we thank Him for it?

Finally in conclusion I want to say that there are two ways to guide someone. One is to give him a map and tell him to follow it. The danger with this is that the person may not understand the map completely, may misinterpret some directions or may not be able to deal with unexpected situations that may arise during his journey and may still not reach the destination even though he had the map. A more sure way to guide the person however is to send someone who knows the way and say, 'Follow him and you will be guided.' That is what Allahﷻ did. He said:

قُلْ أَطِيعُوا اللَّهَ وَأَطِيعُوا الرَّسُولَ فَإِن تَوَلَّوا فَإِنَّمَا عَلَيْهِ مَا حُمِّلَ وَعَلَيْكُم مَّا حُمِّلْتُمْ وَإِن تُطِيعُوهُ تَهْتَدُوا وَمَا عَلَى الرَّسُولِ إِلَّا الْبَلَاغُ الْمُبِينُ

Noor 24: 54. *Say: "Obey Allah and obey the Messenger, but if you turn away, he (Messenger Muhammad) is only responsible for the duty placed on him (i.e. to convey Allah's Message) and you for that placed on you. If you obey him, you shall be on the right guidance. The Messenger's duty is only to convey (the message) in a clear way (i.e. to preach in a plain way)."*

So why didn't Allah ﷻ simply say, 'If you obey Allah ﷻ you will be on right guidance,'? We seem to think that the Sunnah is left to our discretion, to follow or not as we wish. If that were the case Allah ﷻ would not have said with respect to Rasoolullah ﷺ, 'If you obey him you shall be on right guidance.' Obedience to the Messenger ﷺ is a fundamental pillar of

Islam. To obey Rasoolullah ﷺ and to follow his Sunnah is Fardh and we will be held accountable for it. To reiterate this Allah ﷻ said:

مَّنْ يُطِعِ الرَّسُولَ فَقَدْ أَطَاعَ اللَّهَ وَمَن تَوَلَّى فَمَا أَرْسَلْنَاكَ

عَلَيْهِمْ حَفِيظًا

Nisa 4: 80. *He who obeys the Messenger (Muhammad), has indeed obeyed Allah, but he who turns away, then we have not sent you (O Muhammad) as a watcher over them.*

Allah ﷻ also mentioned what He will do in this Dunya for those who obey and follow the Messenger ﷺ. He said:

وَعَدَ اللَّهُ الَّذِينَ آمَنُوا مِنكُمْ وَعَمِلُوا الصَّالِحَاتِ

لَيَسْتَخْلِفَنَّهُم فِي الْأَرْضِ كَمَا اسْتَخْلَفَ الَّذِينَ مِن قَبْلِهِمْ

وَلَيُمَكِّنَنَّ لَهُمْ دِينَهُمُ الَّذِي ارْتَضَى لَهُمْ وَلَيُبَدِّلَنَّهُم مِّن بَعْدِ

خَوْفِهِمْ أَمْنًا يَعْبُدُونَنِي لَا يُشْرِكُونَ بِي شَيْئًا وَمَن كَفَرَ بَعْدَ

ذَلِكَ فَأُوْلَئِكَ هُمُ الْفَاسِقُونَ

Noor 24: 55. *Allah has promised those among you who believe, and do righteous good deeds, that He will certainly grant them succession to (the present rulers) in the earth, as He granted it to those before them, and that He will grant them the authority to practice their religion, that which He has chosen for them (Islam). And He will surely give them in exchange security after their fear (provided) they worship Me and do not associate anything (in* *worship) with Me. But whoever disbelieved after this, they are the Fasiqun (rebellious, disobedient to Allah).*

Obedience to the Messenger ﷺ and following his way – the Sunnah is not only to earn the Aakhira but also to earn power, authority, wealth and influence in the Dunya. Allah ﷻ showed us this in the life of the Sahaba itself where people who were nobody were given victory over the super powers of the time and for more than 1000 years thereafter the flag of Islam dominated the world. It was only when Muslims forgot the reason for their victory and allowed themselves to be corrupted and gave in to the same greed and chasing after Dunya that the rest of the world does, that the responsibility of Khilaafa was taken away from them and they became enslaved.

I remind myself that slavery is a state of mind. Not a state of physical confinement. A nation does not lose its glory and fall until it destroys itself from within. What do you say about a people who have the formula for success but refuse to use it and go around searching for solutions in places where they don't exist. We live in a world that has lost the plot. A world that is full of self-created hardship, suffering, oppression and inequity. A world that refuses to recognize that it is the creator of its own state. Yet we who have the solution, refuse to use it or teach it to others.

I ask Allah ﷻ to give us the Tawfeeq to reflect on His Kalaam and to make Tawba and change our lives so that we may be resurrected with Rasoolullah ﷺ and His Sahaba and be given their company in Jannah. May Allah ﷻ be pleased with you all.

Glossary of Terms

A

A'aimma – Plural of Imam, Leaders

Aakhira – Hereafter

Ahadith – Plural of Hadith

Allahﷻ - The personal name of God. The Arabic script after the English means 'The Glorious

Anbiya – Plural of Nabi, Messengers

Arafa, Day of – First day of Hajj. Named after the plain of Arafa where pilgrims gather

Aqeeda – Beliefs

Arsh – Throne

Asr – Afternoon prayer

Ayah – Sign

Ayaat – Signs *(plural)*

B

Baraka – Blessing

Basmallah -

Bida'at – Introduction of new practices in worship which the Prophetﷺ didn't allow

D

Da'awa – (*lit.*) Invitation

Deen – Way of life

Dhuhr – Mid-day prayer

Dhikr - Remembering Allahﷻ in any permissible way

Dhul Qa'da, Dhul Hijja, Muharram, Rajab – Four sacred months of the Islamic calendar

Dua - Supplication, personal prayer asking Allahﷻ whatever one wants

Dunya – This world

F

Fajr – Dawn prayer

Fardh – Obligatory

Fasaad-fil-Aqeeda – Corruption in belief

G

Ghaib - Unperceivable (wrongly called Unseen)

Gheeba – Backbiting

H

Halaal – Allowed, permitted, permissible

Hadith – Teachings of Rasoolullah ﷺ

Hamd – Highest form of praise

Haraam – Forbidden

Hasanaath – Good deeds

Hijab – curtain or cover, specifically means head covering for women

Huqooq Ullah – The rights of Allah جل جلاله

Huqooq ul Ibaad – The rights of the people

I

Ibadaat – Worship *(plural)* Ibaadah *(Singular)*

Imam – Leader

Imaan – Belief

Isha – Night prayer

J

Jahiliyya – Era of Ignorance that predated Islam

Jannah – Paradise

Jahannam – Hell

Jibreel - Angel Gabriel

Juz – 1 of 30 parts of the Qur'an

K

Kalaam – Speech

Khair – Goodness

Kufr – (*lit.*) To hide. Specifically means Denial of Allahﷻ including denying His attributes, commands, words (Qur'an) or His being (atheism)

Kursi – Throne

Khutba – Lecture

Khilaafa – Islamic government

M

Ma'abood – Creator/Fashioner

Maghrib – Sunset prayer

Maula – Patron, Supporter, Protector

Muttaqi – The one who has Taqwa

Mehr – Bridal gift

Munafiqoon – Plural of Munafiq, Hypocrites

N

Nabi – Messenger

Nafl – Voluntary

Nifaaq – Hypocrisy

Niyyah – Intention

Nusrah – Help

Q

Qari – Reciter

Qudsi, Hadith – Saying of Allah not part of the Qur'an

R

Rabb - Sustainer, Protector, Provider for all needs: One of the names of Allahﷻ

Rabbul-A'alameen – Rabb of the Worlds (All that exists)

Raka'at – Unit of Salah

Ramadan – 9th Month of the Hijri Calendar in which Fasting is prescribed

Rasoolullahﷺ - Muhammad, Messenger of Allahﷻ . The Arabic script after the English means: Peace & Blessings be on him

Ribâ - Bank Interest and other similar gains

Rooh – Soul

Ruboobiyat – The Quality of being Rabb

S

Sahabi – (*singular*) male companion of Rasoolullahﷺ. A Muslim who saw the Prophetﷺ and remained on

Islam until he died. (Sahabiya – Female)

Sahaba – (*plural*) male companions of Rasoolullah ﷺ (Sahabiyaat – Female Plural)

Sahih – Authentic, Correct

Sajda – Prostration in worship

Salah – Prayer

Salaat-ul-Janazah – Funeral prayer

Shafa'at – Intercession

Shaheed – Martyr

Shuhadaa – Plural of Shaheed

Shari'ah – Islamic Law

Shaytaan – Satan

Shifa – Cure

Shirk - Polytheism; joining partners with Allahﷻ in his being, work, actions, attributes or power. Or ascribing divinity to anyone or anything other than Allahﷻ

Shuyookh – Plural of Shaykh, Guide/Mentor/Teacher

Sifaat – Attributes, Qualities

Siraatal Mustaqeem – the Path of Steadfastness, the Path of Guidance, the Path of Righteousness

Sunnah – Teachings, actions, circumstances of Muhammadﷺ which is the second source for Islamic Law

Sura – (literally) Picture. Means chapter in the Qur'an

T

Tahajjud - Prayer in the last part of the night, before dawn

Taqwa – Fear of displeasing the beloved (Allahﷻ)

Taraweeh – Special salah during Ramadan

Tarbiyya – Character building

Tawba – Repentance

Tawfeeq – Guidance

Tawhid – Belief in the Oneness of Allah

Tawhid ul Uloohiya – Belief in

Tawhid ur Ruboobiya – Belief in the Ruboobiyat of Allah

U

Ummah – Community, Group, People

Ummati – Member of Ummah

W

Wada – Farewell

Wahi – Revelation that came to the Prophetﷺ and to all Prophets in any form (including Qur'an)

Walidayn – Parents (Walid – father; Walida – mother)

Z

Zakat – Obligatory charity

Appendix

Is the Qur'an – The Word of God: A Rational Perspective

Asadi, Muhammed A.

"Say: What thing is greatest in testimony? Say: God is witness between you and I, and that this Koran has been inspired in me that I many warn with it you and whomsoever it be conveyed to... (Koran 6:19)"

Religion throughout the history of humankind has had a tremendous hold on humanity. According to Emile Durkheim, the French

Sociologist, the first organized institutions of mankind were religious in character. Even today, religion is of primary importance to millions of individuals who try to live by it and give it a special place in their lives. Therefore, any issue involving religion in today's world is worthy of discussion. Science, in its popular usage, is generally defined as the systematic observation of natural phenomena and their workings. Since the industrial revolution in the eighteenth century it is seen as the thing in control of human destiny and its future survival. Those who fail to utilize science and modern discovery are kept at the lowest strata of society in today's highly competitive world.

As today, both science and religion are widespread, each having dogmatic believers, antagonism has resulted. The common notion being that science and religion are opposites; i.e. they repel each other as like poles of a magnet. According to the sociologist Max Weber, in his article, Science as a vocation, science has resulted in the "disenchantment" of the world. The enchantment of the world was due to, according to him, people relying on religion and giving magical explanations to perfectly logical, natural phenomena.

This article attempts to use the Koran to examine Max Weber's claims about religion. The source of Islam is a book, just one book, the Koran. Modern Islam however has added other sources, which the Koran doesn't validate. The Koran, is historically the earliest written text we possess in the the Arabic language and as such is the only valid authority on Islam as conveyed by the prophet Muhammed. The other sources Hadith and Fiqh date from over 200 years after Muhammed's death. I will therefore not deal with these other sources as they do not historically represent the "original" Islam.

Within its text, the Koran names itself many times as a book revealed directly by God, in which God is speaking in the first person. The Koran says that true believers "reason about the origin of the heavens and the earth (Koran 3:190-191)." This itself is science by definition when done in a systematic way. According to the Koran, by applying science in this way a person gets to the truth by discovering the "nature of God [His Sunna- in Arabic]," as reflected by his creation and brought to mind by the Koran that claims to be his revelation. In contrast to the concept of a "supernatural", the Koran talks about nature and creation being an expression of God's attributes. We can therefore look inside the "Mind of God" so to speak by studying his creation.

The scientific system of inquiry is emphasized time and again by the Koran. The linking of science and rationality with the verses of the Koran is not only legitimized but also encouraged by God in the Koran. The Koran tells the reader that if he/she does not know something or are unsure they should ask "those who are informed (Koran 25:59)."

In the case of all the scientific and natural phenomena discussed in the Koran, the people having knowledge and information would most definitely be the scientists. **Thus the Koran discourages unreasoned belief.**

Why I came to be interested in the scientific analysis of the Koran, is a long story that traverses my entire life after thirteen. It was at that age, while going through my father's closet, in the process of moving to a different city in Pakistan, that I discovered several English translations of the Koran. I was curious about this book. I had heard its name being raised in a so called "Islamic environment," yet no one ever told me what the book was about. In the society in which I grew up, most people claim to be Muslims, but they never read the Koran in a language they understand. They merely chant it in Arabic, which they have learned to read mechanically, but whose meaning they don't know. It would sound very unusual here, to the American culture, to be able to read in English but not understand a word of it. No one asked me to read the book, I read it because its daily reading made sense to me. It motivated me to question and I could confirm it with the little knowledge that I had from school at that time.

As time progressed, discussions with the people I met raised many questions regarding religion and its relation to science and reason. A human mind can never rest on uncertainty and so till I succeeded in my attempts to find answers to questions that arose in my mind, I was always restless. The attitude that I carry with me even today, after over thirteen years of extensive research is that the day I find a confirmed scientific error in the Koran, I'll stop believing in it. Objectivity and concern for value-free truth demands that. I have yet to find one though, so I consider myself a Muslim at present. This attitude is encouraged by the Koran itself when it challenges people to find errors in it. In my daily life, whenever I read the Koran, I read it critically, trying to analyse it objectively; by doing so I'm following Koran 4:82:

"Do they not carefully consider the Koran. If it had been from anyone other than God, they would have found in it many contradictions."

If the Koran is indeed the word of the Creator, as it claims to be (Koran 4:166), then it must be error-free when it discusses details about proven facts of science, like description of stages in embryology. The Koran claims, to originate from the one who has "knowledge of everything" (Koran 20:98). Thus it implies complete accuracy.

The Koran encourages verifying its claims when it presents information. For example, the details about embryology in the Koran are presented in a fashion that would facilitate belief only after those verses have been checked by known findings. They are presented as a challenge: ***"If you are in doubt then (consider this).... (22:5 etc)"***

The same is also witnessed throughout the Koran when the book makes statements like,

"Do you not know.... (Or) Have you not seen and considered etc." Also consider all the falsification tests contained in the Koran, like the one which challenges people to produce a chapter comparable to the Book (Koran 2:23). All these legitimize and encourage a rational/scientific inquiry into the truthfulness of the Koran.

Maurice Bucaille, one of the first to popularize the linking of the Koran and Science, in his best selling books, The Bible, the Koran and Science, and What is the Origin of Man, concluded that given the history of the origin of the Koran, it could not have been the work of a man or group of men living in Arabia or anywhere else at that time, considering the nature of the scientific information in the Koran. Lecturing at the French Academy of Medicine, he concluded on the subject:

"It makes us deem it quite unthinkable for a man of Muhammed's time to have been the author of such statements on account of the state of knowledge in his day. Such considerations are what give the Koranic revelation its unique place and forces the

impartial scientist to admit his inability to provide an explanation which calls solely on materialistic reasoning."(Bucaille 1985)

Keith Moore, head of the department of anatomy, at the University of Toronto, was shown verses of the Koran dealing with the microscopic stages of the human embryo. He was so surprised at what he found that he went back and revised the history of embryology in his standard texts on the subject. The books that Keith Moore authored are used at prestigious institutions like Yale and at universities all around the world. He stated, after being unable to provide an explanation on how microscopic details of the embryo could be accurately described in a book written before the discovery of the microscope:

"It is clear to me that these statements (in the Koran on embryology) must have come to Muhammad from God. This proves to me that Muhammed must have been the messenger of God or Allah." (Rehaili 1995)

Consider yourself an inhabitant of 7th Century Arabia. Society has very little scientific knowledge. Myth and magic control people's thoughts. How far would you go if you wanted to discover the true origin or the universe? How much progress would you make if you wanted to uncover the origin of life? We can move away from Arabia and scan the world scene at that period in history. Nothing in the literature of the world comes even remotely close to the scientific accuracy of statements about the natural world contained in the Koran. In fact some of the information that we come across in the Koran wasn't known till about 40 years back and some of it wasn't known until the day it was read in the Koran by scientists just a few years ago.

Since the Koran claims to originate with the one (God) who originated everything (Koran 55:2), and has knowledge of everything (Koran 20:98), we have every right to logically inquire if the originator of the earth and the heavens, in the knowledge that he gives us about them knows what we have discovered about their origin through modern science. The Koran can thus be scientifically tested in order to verify its claims.

The Koran exists in the world today. Therefore,

if we do not accept the book's claim of being a revelation, then we must come up with an explanation as to its origin. The existence of the Koran cannot be denied. If we choose to deny it then we need to at least present a sound explanation to justify denial.

People who reject the Koran's claim throughout the ages have come up with explanations and theories as to the origin of the Koran.

No matter what the details of the particular theory might be, they all reduce to basically two hypothesis:

i) ***Muhammad was a liar.*** He got his information from the outside and presented it to people as a revelation from God. The proponents of this hypothesis claim that the Koran was composed by Muhammad who "borrowed" information from other sources. Some even suggest that Muhammad was helped by a "group" of people to compose the Koran.

ii) The second hypothesis suggests that ***Muhammed was deceived or deluded*** in that he believed that he was a prophet when in fact he was not. To the people who offer this hypothesis, the Koran is the product of the "deluded" mind of Muhammed. Muhammad's hallucinations.

It may sound surprising but the book that is being attacked, the Koran, is also well aware of these two hypothesis that people have been presenting throughout the ages in trying to reject it:

Hypothesis 1 suggests that Muhammad was a liar. The Koran states:

"They (the rejecters) say: 'These are tales of the ancients, which he has caused to be written down so that they are dictated to him morning and evening (Koran 5:25)."

Hypothesis 2 suggests that Muhammed was self-deceived. The Koran states:

"The ones who reject almost trip you up by

glaring at you when they hear The Reminder (Koran), and they say,' He is indeed deranged (Koran 68:51).''

Most people who present these hypotheses are forced to take them together in conjunction. Logically speaking however, both these hypothesis are mutually exclusive and cannot be taken together. They can stand on their own, if facts support them, but taken together they collapse. As an example: If a man is a liar (Hypothesis 1) then when someone asks the man a question, he has to search for the answer. He looks either within himself for the answer or asks his friends in secrecy so that he can give the inquirer a satisfactory response. He knows that he is not a prophet so he has to lie to convince the questioner. On the other hand, if the man is deluded (Hypothesis 2) then when someone asks the man a question, he does not search for the answer, if he doesn't know it. He is deluded, self-deceived, he believes he is a prophet and the answer will be given to him by revelation.

To repeat the above, if the man is a liar, he knows he is not a prophet and investigation can provide evidence as to where the material came from, but if he is deluded, even though the material presented is his own hallucinations, still he cannot be termed a liar for he believes he is a prophet. If a man is a liar then he is not self-deceived, if he is self-deceived then he is not a liar. Therefore Hypothesis 1 and Hypothesis 2 cannot be mixed up in explaining the Koran. However, what we see is that people need both excuses to explain certain things in the Koran. They often start by presenting Hypothesis 1 (Muhammed was a liar) and end up with Hypothesis 2 (Muhammed was self-deceived), i.e. Muhammed was a liar and self-deceived.

This cannot be, logically speaking as we have seen above.

It may again surprise you but the Koran is also aware of this illogical stand that people take by terming Muhammad both a liar and self deluded. The Koran states:

" And they have turned away and said, 'One taught (by others), and a madman (44:14).").

The Koran can be Hypothesis (1) i.e. the product of a liar, or Hypothesis (2) i.e. the product of a deceived mind, or it can be what it claims to be, i.e. God's revelation; but it can never be both Hypothesis 1 and Hypothesis 2 at the same time.

Hypothesis 1 and its implications: If the Koran is the product of a man's mind who is a "liar", who got his information from the outside and then presented it to the world as a revelation then:

1. We have to explain the confidence portrayed by the various statements in the Koran. A confidence that shows that whosoever is presenting this is convinced that he indeed has the truth. As examples: a) The Koran

challenges people to find a mistake in the book by its claim that if God was not the author many mistakes would be found in it (Koran4:82) Now only a person who is convinced about what he has can make such a claim. Do you know of any book that makes a claim that it doesn't contain any errors and that if it had a human origin it would contain many. The Bible never makes such a claim.

b) Another example would be the invitation given to Christians who dispute with Muslims about the nature of Jesus as presented in the Koran. The verse says:

"Come let us call our sons and your sons...our families and your families and let us ask God to curse the ones who are lying (about the true information on Jesus) (Koran 3:61)."

This shows that whoever is presenting this is confident and sure that he has the truth on which the challenge is based.

c) Another example of this **confidence** that a liar is incapable of portraying, is the account of when the Meccans who wanted to kill Muhammad came unto the mouth of the cave in which he and his friend Abu-Bakr were hiding. Abu-Bakr was afraid, Muhammed told him to "relax", "God will save us," he told him. Now if the man is a liar, one who lies to convince people that he is a prophet, you might expect him to say, "Go and look for a back way out," or "lie low and be quiet." But what he actually said shows that he had no doubt that he was a prophet and that God would save them. Hypothesis 1 cannot explain these in the Koran.

2. If the Koran is a lie, the product of a man's lying mind, how do you account for the following: The Koran claims that it contains information that was "new" to the people it was being read to. Now the Meccans hated Muhammad, if this statement in the Koran was not true and the information was not "new" they would have loved to point out the source. Yet they never answered this challenge to produce similar "knowledge" as the Koran (chapter 46: verse 4)

As proof of the above, I'll give two examples:

1. The Koran mentions the wall of "Zulqarnain," the two-horned one. It gives a

complete description of this wall and how it was built to protect a people from outside invaders (Koran 18:96-98). The Arabs had never heard of it, or what it looked like, neither had the Arab Jews or the Arab Christians. Now, after the death of the prophet, they were curious about this wall mentioned in the Koran. Omar the Khalif sent out travelers to verify the existence of this wall. It is in Durbent in the former Soviet Union. It is referred to as Alexander's wall however modern historians dispute on whether Alexander had anything to do with it.

Compare what the Koran said over fourteen centuries back, before any Arab had set foot on Derbent to what the Columbia Encyclopaedia says:

"Derbent was founded (A.D 438) by the Persians as a strategic fortress at the Iron Gates. There are remains of the Caucasian Wall (also called Alexander's Wall), built by the Persians in the 6th century. as a bulwark against northern invaders. (6th Edition, 2000)."

If Muhammed was a liar, who told him about this wall thousands of miles to the east, about which no one in his area knew anything?

2. The Koran mentions a city by the name of Iram where a prosperous people the AAD lived. It was a city of "tall pillars":

"Have you seen how your sustainer (God)

dealt with the Aad people? Iram, of the lofty pillars (Koran 89:8-8)"

Until very recently no historic or non-historic record existed about Iram. However in 1973, the ancient city of Ebla was excavated in Syria. While going through the tablet library of Ebla archaeologists came across a list of cities that Ebla traded with and on that list was a city named Iram. When reporting it in the National Geographic of December 1978, the only reference to Iram they could cite other than the tablets was the Koran, chapter 89.

In 1992 using SIR-C imaging [Synthetic Aperture Radar] using the Space Shuttle, GPR [Ground Penetrating Radar] and GMT [Geophysical Diffraction Tomography], scientists discovered Iram [also called Ubar] in southern Oman, buried under 12 meters of sand. The city contained evidence of "tall pillars" exactly as mentioned in the Koran chapter 89. The Koran described this fact, over fourteen centuries back at a time when no one in the world could have had access to this city. Now, if Muhammad was a liar where did he get this information?

Hypothesis 2 and its implications:

Hypothesis 2 suggests that the Koran is the product of a man's deluded mind. If the Koran is a product of a man's hallucinations then what comes out as a result are things that are in his mind. What do you think went on in

Muhammed's mind? He didn't have an easy life.

He was an orphan to start with, then his grandfather who looked after him died, then his uncle who adopted him died as well. After that, his life companion, his wife of 24 years Khatija died. All his children except for one daughter died in his lifetime. Does the Koran reflect any of this? It doesn't even mention these things at all. Yet these were the things that surely bothered him and caused him pain through his whole life, but they never show up in a book, which is said to be the product of his deluded mind!

In fact, the information contained in the Koran is such that no man living anywhere in the 7th century could have known it. I'll give some examples, which should make the point clear:

1. THE ORIGIN OF LIFE

The Koran mentions that all life originated from water (Koran 21:30) and that man himself is "created" of water and so are all the animals on earth (Koran 25:54, and 24:45). Now these statements to an Arab would have sounded atrocious in that day and age. Even today such statements in the Koran might cause you to wonder if scientific facts about them are unknown. The fact that all life originated in water is well established by the scientific community today. They have evidence to support the fact that the first living beings were algae, and they existed in water. The fact that human beings and animals are created of water is also well established since cytoplasm the basic component of "life" in any animal cell is over 80% water.

2. **MATURITY**

The Koran mentions that a human being reaches full maturity at age forty (Koran 46:15). This is a very unusual statement. Even today most people accept that full maturity is reached at puberty and laws usually put it between 18 to 21. However, the Koran is scientifically correct where even modern laws are inaccurate. If we analyze the statement based on psychological tests conducted by scientisits, what we find is that the "overall quantity of stored knowledge in the mind of an individual reaches a peak at age thirty-nine and after that it gradually declines." Arthur C.

Guyton, in his standard textbook on physiology, Physiology of the Human Body(6th ed, pg.207), states this. Guyton's book is used as a standard text in at many pre-medical schools around the world.

3. **THE FEMALE BEE**

The Koran mentions the bee, which leaves its home in search for food, in the verses that discusses honey (Koran 16:68,69). It uses the female verb in describing the bee, in Arabic faslukee. This, to the Arab, suggests that the bee, which leaves its home in search for food, is female.

Does anyone except an expert know how to differentiate between a male and a female bee? Even today, let alone Muhammad's time, 1400 plus years back, we need a specialist to differentiate between a male and a female bee. The Koran is accurate when it mentions that the female bee leaves its home in search for food; the males never leave their homes for food, it is the females who have to feed them.

4. EMBRYO SEX DETERMINATION

The Koran says that the "**ejaculated drop**" determines the sex of a human baby (Koran 53:45). It is common knowledge that semen is the fluid that is ejaculated by males during sexual acts. Females do not possess such "ejaculated semen."

The sex of the baby, whether it be male or

female, will indeed be determined by the 'ejaculated drop', i.e. the father's sperm, as mentioned by the Koran. It has been scientifically established only recently that the female ovum contains only X-chromosomes. If the ejaculated drop, the father's sperm bears the Y chromosome, the offspring will be male, and otherwise the offspring will be female. No one living at the time of Muhammed or even Darwin for that matter had any knowledge of such genetics foretold centuries earlier in the Koran.

5. **THE INVISIBLE BARRIER**

The Koran states that there are two seas that meet but don't intermingle because of a barrier between them (Koran 55:19-20).

It is a necessity that seas intermingle through straits between them. The Koran however is aware of a very unusual phenomenon, which scientists discovered only recently. The Mediterranean and Atlantic oceans differ in their chemical and biological constitution. The French scientist Jacques Yves Cousteau conducted various undersea investigations at the Strait of Gibraltar and explaining these phenomena concluded:

"Unexpected fresh water springs issue from the southern and northern coasts of Gibraltar. These mammoth springs gush towards each other at angles of 45 degrees forming a reciprocal dam. Due to this fact the Mediterranean and the Atlantic Oceans cannot intermingle (as quoted by Nurbaki)."

Did Muhammed do research on the chemical and biological components of seawater to discover this unusual phenomena?

6. **THE GASEOUS ORIGIN OF THE UNIVERSE**

The Koran mentions that the universe originated, at a stage, from a "gaseous material." (Koran 41:11). It uses the Arabic word Dukhan, which stands for smoke. A perfect analogy for gas and particles in suspension and the gasses being hot.

Scientists have only very recently confirmed that the universe did indeed originate from a gaseous mass composed of hydrogen and helium, a big mass of hot gasses, a mass over

300,000 times that of the earth. That mass then fragmented to form galaxies. Muhammad, who had no schooling of any kind and was illiterate before the revelation of the Koran, could not have possibly known this.

7. THE BIG BANG

The Koran gives an accurate visual description of the Big Bang theory of the creation of the universe. In the 21st chapter, verse 30 (21:30), the Koran states:

"Do not the rejecters see that the heavens and earth were a unit joined together then we split them apart (21:30)."

This is exactly how the 'rejecter' scientists envision the creation of the universe, from one singularity, which then exploded, termed the 'big bang'. Thus the Koran told us about the "common origin" of everything in the universe much before scientists described it in the 20th century. How do we explain this information in the Koran if it is not what it claims to be, the words of an all-knowing ?

Professor Alfred Kroner, chairman of the Department of Geology at the Institute of Geosciences, Johannes Gutenburg University, Mainz, Germany stated about this verse in the Koran:

"Somebody who did not know something about nuclear physics 1400 years ago could not, I think, be in a position to find out from his own mind for instance that the earth and the heavens had the same origin, or many others of the questions that we have discussed here.(Rehaili 1995)"

8. **THE EXPANDING UNIVERSE**

The Koran talks about a universe that is continually "expanding" (Koran 51:47).

The concept of an expanding universe is very popular with scientists today, however no one knew of it until recently. Do you know that the universe is expanding? Can you feel or see it expanding? No, the verification of this requires specialized knowledge and instruments, which no one at the time of Muhammad had access to. The Koran states:

"And the sky we built it with might and We

cause the 'expansion' of it (Koran 51:47)."

9. **THE DEATH OF STARS**

The Koran mentions the 'death of stars' (Koran 77:7-8). Astronomers including Dr. Patterson of Southwest Missouri State are surprised at finding this information in the Koran. They know that at the time of Muhammad, people believed that once a thing was formed, it was permanent. The Koran is very accurate when it mentions dying stars. Our own sun is a dying star.

10. **PHASES OF THE MOON**

The Koran talks about the phases of the moon (Koran 36:38-39). There is no book, to my knowledge, that predates the Koran that mentions the modern term "phase" in connection with the moon. Dr. Patterson confirms this. The Arabic word used for "phase" in the Koran is Manazil.

11. MOVEMENT OF THE SUN

The sun's movement is not something that is evident to our eyes or experience but requires specialized equipment. The Koran states in chapter 36, verse 39:

"And the sun constantly journeys towards a homing place for it and for the moon, We have determined phases (36:39)."

Modern science has found out that the sun rotates around its axis every 26 days . The Koran mentions the movement of the sun, with its own motion, signified by the verb

Yasbahoon in Arabic. Thus according to the Koran the sun is not just flying through space but moving on its own, i.e. rotating. The sun is also continually on a journey in space towards its homing place, the solar apex, just like mentioned in the Koran (36:39). How could Muhammed have known these facts if the Koran is the product of his mind?

12. **ISOSTACY AND MOUNTAIN ROOTS**

The Koran states that mountains are like "tent-pegs", i.e. they have a root extending down into the earth like "anchors" and this gives stability and balance to the earth.

"Have we not expanded the earth and made the mountains as tent pegs" (Koran 78:6-7)
" We have cast into the earth anchors lest it

shake with you" (Koran 31:10 etc.) This fact was discovered less than 150 years ago by scientists and now accepted as a fundamental law in geology, the concept of isostacy. M. J Selby in a standard-text on the subject entitled "Earth's Changing Surface (Clarendon Press, Oxford 1985) states:

"G.B Airy in 1855 suggested that the crust of the earth could be likened to rafts of timber floating on water. Thick pieces of timber float higher above the water surface than thin pieces and similarly thick sections of the earth's crust will float on a liquid or plastic substratum of greater density. Airy was suggesting that mountains have a deep root of lower density rock, which the plains lack. Four years after Airy published his work, J.H Pratt offered an alternative hypothesis...By this hypothesis, rock columns below mountains must have a lower density, because of their greater length, than shorter rock columns beneath plains. Both Airy and Pratt's hypothesis imply that surface irregularities are balanced by differences in density of rocks below the major features (mountains and plains) of the crust. This state of BALANCE is described as the concept of ISOSTACY (Selby1985:32)."

13. HUMAN EMBRYOLOGY

The Koran is known to be the first book to give microscopic details of human embryology(Koran 23:13-14 etc.), hundreds of years before the discovery of the microscope! The Koran contains information on embryology, which was not discovered till about 30 years back and certain details were new even to modern scientists but were immediately confirmed as being accurate.

The Koran mentions that at a certain stage, the developing human is like "allaqa", a leech-like clot. If you take a microscopic picture of a human embryo of days 7-12 and place it next to a picture of a leech, they both look identical. Not only do they look the same but they function in the same way too. Just like a leech derives nourishment from its host's blood, the embryo derives nourishment from the decidua or the pregnant endometrium. These facts about the Koran are well documented and listed by Keith L. Moore in his standard textbooks on embryology, books used in such prestigious institutions as the Yale Medical School.

14. RESURRECTION OF THE DEAD

"Nay! I swear by the day of resurrection. Nay! I swear by the reproachful self (Super Ego?).
Does man think that We shall not gather his bones?
Yea! We are able to make complete his very fingertips....
.....What, does humankind think that they will be left to roam at will? Was he not a drop ejaculated? Then he was a leech-like structure. And He (God) created and formed. And made of him a pair, the male and the female

. What, is He (God) then not able to quicken the dead?" Koran 75:1-40

The above verse of the Koran questions those who reject the notion of the resurrection of the dead. What is the more difficult task: That you were created from an insignificant drop, which was so small that it couldn't be seen except through a microscope, or that one day you will be formed from your remnants?

Russian scientists recently discussed reproducing an extinct species of elephant by use of a microscopic unit of long-dead gene material. No one in the scientific community said that that was unreasonable. The point is that the resurrection of the dead might be an unusual think but it certainly is not unreasonable. The use of cloning techniques throws further light on the amazing nature of the Koranic verse which compares the resurrection of the dead with human development from an insignificant zygote to the fetus. Cloning provides theoretic and empirical evidence for the resurrection of the dead.

15. CIRCULATION OF BLOOD AND FOOD

"And surely in the cattle, there is a lesson for you. We give you to drink of what is inside their bodies, from between digested food and blood, pure milk, pleasant to those who drink it (Koran 16:6)."

The above verse of the Koran calls our attention to the food distribution function of blood. It should be kept in mind however that a Muslim scientist formally discovered the circulation of blood 600 years after Muhammed's death and it was made known to the west by William Harvey, 1000 years after Muhammed had died. If Muhammed was the author of the Koran how would he have known, at the time that he lived that digested food is transported via blood and then becomes the constituent of milk secreted by the mammary glands?

16. THE "CONSTANTS" AND THE INITIAL CONDITIONS

"Do they [the disbelievers] not see that God has subjected for them whatsoever is in the heavens and on earth (Koran 31:20)? " Indeed We have created everything with a set measure

(Koran 54:49)

Compare these statements in the Koran to what the physicist Paul Davies writes in his book, The Accidental Universe (1982):

"The numerical values that nature has assigned to the fundamental constants, such as the charge on the electron, the mass of the proton, and the Newtonian Gravitational constant, may be mysterious, but they are critically relevant to the structure of the universe that we perceive. As more and more physical systems from nuclei to galaxies have become better understood, scientists have begun to realize that many characteristics of these systems are remarkably sensitive to the precise value of the fundamental constants. Had nature opted for a slightly different set of numbers, the world would have been a very different place and we would not be here to see it." (Davies 1982)

At around 300,000 years after the big bang, all parts of the universe, even separated by more than 20 times the horizon distance, and expanding in opposite directions, in causally disconnected regions (i.e.. no cause or physical effect could pass from one region to the other), began to expand with the same expansion rate and temperature.

No natural explanation exists to explain how a chaotic explosion, the big bang resulted in a uniform expansion pattern among causally disconnected regions, expanding in opposite directions. Calculations indicate that when the universe was less than a trillionth of a second old, it consisted of 10 to the power 80 causally disconnected regions, and no physical effect could have traveled from one region to another and yet 300,000 years after, cosmic background radiation proves that they all started expanding with the same expansion rate and the same temperature. It was as if they acted upon uniformly communicated intelligent direction. Consider what the Koran says:

"... And He (God) inspired in all the heavens their affair (Koran 41:12)."

The "Flatness" or "smoothness" of the universe is established by modern science and leads scientists to wonder as to how a uniform distribution of matter resulted from the big bang. The Koran is aware of this and presents the "smoothness" of the universe as a challenge to unbelievers:

"[It is God] who has created the multiple skies, one separate from the other (as layers). You cannot see any flaw in the Merciful (God's) creation. Look again, can you make out any rifts?"(Koran 67:3)

If we deny the Koran's claim of being God's revelation, we have to account for the above information, and how it made its way into the Koran, always without error, and always accurate. Justice and truth demand that or we are fooling ourselves alone.

(B)FALSIFICATION TESTS

The Koran offers what is not offered by religions, generally speaking. It offers what the scientific community demands before they even listen to any new theory, falsification tests. The Koran presents itself with tests to disprove it, if it is false.

¨ The Koran in 4:82 challenges people to find a mistake or contradiction in the book and hence disqualify it, if it is indeed a lie.

¨ The Koran talks about people and how they will behave. If they were to act contrary to how the Koran pre-told their behavior, it would be disqualified.

Muhammad had an uncle by the name of Abu-Lahab. This man hated Muhammad and was always strong in opposing him. Many years before the man died, the small chapter in the Koran documented his behavior, saying that he will be condemned and will never change (Koran 111:1-5). All he had to do to prove the Koran wrong was say: "I am a Muslim, I change my behavior, your book is wrong." Yet he never did do it, never thought of it even though he would have loved to.

¨ The Koran claims that in a pluralistic society, the Christians would always treat the Muslims better than the Jews and Idolaters (Koran 5:85,86).

Scan the world scene where Jews, Christians and Muslims live together. Are the Jews closer to the Muslims or the Christians? The only thing the Jews have to do to disprove the Koran is to band together and treat the Muslims better than the Christians do for a little while and the Koran is disproved. However this has not happened yet.

¨ The Koran says that if it is not what it claims to be then people should produce a document comparable to it (Koran 2:23 etc).

Comparison criteria would be what I have discussed earlier: **i)** It should contain information, which no one knows today, but will be found out tomorrow as scientifically accurate. **ii)** It should contain falsification tests as the Koran. **iii)** It should stand the test of "forgery" and "hallucination" as the Koran does. **iv)** It should give "sound" scientifically testable social advice as the Koran. **v)** Equal the

Koran on literary merits. **vi)** Should have God speaking in the first person as the Koran does and then pass the test of inerrancy.

In the face of all the facts that the Koran provides, it is evident that it challenges human intellect and explanation and presents itself as a challenge to traditional religion and skeptical scientists. In the light of this, let us consider this claim that it makes:

If all of humankind and the other intelligent life were to band together to produce the like of this Koran, they would not be able to, even if they backed up each other with help and support (Koran 17:89).

REFERENCES

1. Miller, Gary. The Amazing Quran. (Video Recording, transcribed, Sept 1990, Asadi, Muhammed. Lahore, Pakistan).

2. Asadi, Muhammed A. 1992. Koran: A Scientific Analysis. Lahore. Pakistan.

3. Asadi, Muhammed A. 1995. The Message of Qur'an and Islam. Lahore, Pakistan: Ferozsons' Ltd.

4. Asadi, Muhammed A. 2000. The Unifying Theory of Everything: Koran & Nature's Testimony.Writer's Club Press. New York.

5. Koran. Translated from the Arabic.

6. Maurice. What is the Origin of Man? 1987. Seghers, Paris.

7. Bucaille, Maurice. The Bible, the Qur'an and Science. 1985. Seghers. Paris.

8. Rehaili. Abdullah. M. This is the Truth. 1995.

Riyadh. Saudi Arabia.

Printed in Great Britain
by Amazon

39416207R00109